Endorsements

"This is the best business book I have read since *Good to Great*. It is rare to find an author that can convey such extensive experience and learning in such a compelling and effective way."

—Dave Daniels, Owner Double D Consulting and Former VP of Operations, Sport Clips, Inc.

"A seasoned professional with a rich array of free enterprise corporate experience … an informed and insightful view of organizations, their people and leaders at their best—and worst. A refreshing gem!"

—Charles G. Zeisser, Former Vice President of Human Resources SSM Health Care of Wisconsin

"Juan is a true North for those who enter the Corporate arena in a way that combines experience with humor … he tells it like it is, from the heart, with style, and right on target (just as he did as a Warrior). This is a must-read several times throughout your career as you deal with Barbarians, and you will …"

—Brian Unger, Former Chief Operating Officer, Einstein Noah Restaurant Group, Inc.

"I can't imagine anyone more qualified to write a book about Warriors. Juan has seen it all, from very poor leadership environments/cultures to the very best corporate America has to offer. Any reader of this book will certainly come away with stories and gems to further their careers."

—David L. Thomas, Former Co-Principal and Executive Officer, LCA Vision

"Juan Marcos is one of the most strategic, insightful, humble and straightforward leaders I have ever had the pleasure of knowing. I am thrilled that he is now sharing his gifts for all to read in this book."

—STEVE RUSSELL, SENIOR VICE PRESIDENT, HUMAN RESOURCES, McDONALD'S CORP.

"Juan has always used his wisdom, talent and intelligence to do what's right in life and in business. Whether you are a leader or a subordinate, his book is a blueprint on how to succeed in the business of people."

—JOHN DECARRIER, McDONALD'S FRANCHISEE

"Juan has captured one of life's most important lessons: 'TEACH OTHERS to READ.' In life, it is not only about reading a book, but also reading the actions of others. In business, as in life, we are constantly learning what to do, not to do, what to say, don't say, and when to give praise – or not. Juan, thanks for sharing the stories that can help some of us learn to *read* at a faster pace."

—CODY TEETS, VICE PRESIDENT AND GENERAL MANAGER, McDONALD'S CORPORATION AND AUTHOR OF *GOLDEN OPPORTUNITY: REMARKABLE CAREERS THAT BEGAN AT McDONALD'S*

WARRIORS

A LEADER'S GUIDE TO

AT THE

SUCCESS IN BUSINESS

HELM

JUAN CARLOS MARCOS

Dedication

With admiration to all the Warriors who toil in corporations, this book is dedicated to your spirit and all you do to make your enterprises successful. You are the heart of what makes corporations and the capitalist free-enterprise economic system the best in the world.

Foreword

One of the many stories surrounding the 2014 Super Bowl was that the two head coaches of the competing teams had been head coaches of another NFL team in the past. Their respective earlier tenures did not end well. They both were fired for not achieving the results that they were expected to achieve, which was to win football games and get into the playoffs. I believe that both of these coaches learned valuable lessons the first time around that helped them to lead differently, prepare differently, and cope differently the second time around and ultimately lead their new teams to the world-championship game.

Early in my career, after a challenging presentation that did not go well, a senior executive in attendance wrote in my presentation deck, "pain is growth." Whether you're leading a football team, parenting or navigating the turbulent waters of corporate America, you will inevitably be feeling the pain that seemingly is the by-product of growth. How can you minimize that pain and accelerate your learning?

After four years of college and maybe a graduate degree, those entering the high-velocity world of business quickly recognize that this unique world is not about theories or, necessarily, linear thinking. It's about getting ahead of an ever-changing consumer, challenging motivated competitors, surviving legislative threats, working through the barriers that internal bureaucracies create every day and, most importantly, accountability. Where do you learn about that?

Whether you're just getting started, or you are a thirty-year warrior, nothing is as valuable to your growth and for preparing you for success as learning through trial and error. However, modern-day corporate America can be very unforgiving or impatient through your learning process.

This book represents the next best thing to being there, which is learning from others' experience. Juan Marcos has provided the reader with a practical tool that offers valuable insights into the distinctive and real differences between effective leaders (those who people eagerly follow) and those who lack the self-awareness to understand that they may be barriers to progress versus a catalyst. To further add texture to his insights, Juan elicits and shares thoughts from veteran executives who share personal experiences and perspectives derived from years of trench warfare.

In the period of time that I worked directly with Juan, he was an invaluable business partner. He never deviated from true north. He abhorred politics and was always about doing the right thing, not the easy thing. When the bureaucracy would interfere with focusing on the customer and the business, Juan would assume a "super hero" persona who I lovingly called "the Cuban." His passion and point of view was on full display, telling you what you may not want to hear but always being relentless in working toward positive change.

This book will, perhaps, serve as a mirror reflecting some of the traits and behaviors that may be derailing your career. Or, it can help you fine-tune some of your positive attributes. Better yet, if you're just getting started in the business world, it will provide you with the awareness and knowledge of the life "on the inside" that will help you emulate and demonstrate the behaviors that will keep your career on a positive and productive track.

Those of us who are given the privilege to lead others have an obligation to be self-aware and eager to continue to challenge the status quo that we may find ourselves mired in. With this book, you have the benefit of having access to "the Cuban" and his breadth of real-world business experience, keen observation skills, and knowledge and understanding of the human condition to help capture what a lifetime of business experience can teach you without, perhaps, the accompanying pain.

Mike Andres
Chairman and Chief Executive Officer, Logan's Roadhouse Inc.

Introduction

Corporate America gets my utmost respect. I believe there is no better capitalistic machine on the planet. Further, being an avowed supporter of capitalism, I accept it all, including its faults. Capitalism is tough and unforgiving. If you snooze, you lose. If you get too insular or self-absorbed, you lose. The quickest route to the graveyard is to stop listening to customers or take them for granted. Another slower form of death is to stop listening to employees. But I challenge you to show me a better model for creating jobs, wealth, education and prosperity.

That being said, many of the perspectives that I'll share in this book will not be kind to the corporate world. I'm sure there are some who will judge my assessments to be irreverent. So be it. My intention is to share my perspectives and experiences, and those of colleagues, for the reader to use as a guide to navigate the corporate world.

My primary intention is to share views I believe are held by many but expressed by few. The second is to provide readers with ideas on how to navigate through corporations, including their careers. Though corporations can be frustrating, trust that you are not unique about your feelings and that you also are not alone in your desire to succeed without becoming a Barbarian.

Yes, the corporate arena and business in general are challenging and deserve to be taken seriously. This point of view does not, however, dictate that people take themselves and their circumstances seriously all the time. A bit of fun and irreverence is good, in my opinion, and served me well throughout my career. Accordingly, my irreverence is not intended to disrespect; rather, it is to spotlight that corporate life is, as is real life, too short and not too be taken so seriously that it makes the journey unbearable.

The primary focus of this book is people, even though I will delve into other topics that shed light on how challenging institutions can be. It is people, after all, who create organizations, shape corporate cultures and define business strategies. And it is mostly people who determine whether enterprises thrive or fail. Though my inspiration to write this book was primarily to cull the behaviors of the people who make corporations more challenging than they need to be—the Dumb Asses and Egomaniacs, aka Barbarians—I will also share observations and perspectives on the great people who populate companies. These are the people I refer to as Warriors.

There are many reasons companies fail or become a shell of what they once were. There are an equal number of reasons companies succeed or overcome major challenges. If you dissect either the failures or successes, the common denominator is people. Jim Collins, in his book *Good to Great*,[1] identified the critical attributes of great and enduring leaders and some of their key people practices. It is an interesting read and refreshingly straightforward for a business book. At the other end of the spectrum, there is much to be learned about the egos and personal dynamics of leaders in companies such as Enron,[2] Tyco[3] and WorldCom,[4] to name a few of recent infamy. Regarding the latter, have you ever asked yourself: "How did that person ever ascend to such a top role in the organization?"

My background in Corporate America spanned over 37 years. It includes experience in industries spanning health care, manufacturing, and restaurants. My entire professional career was spent in human resources, but at times I also dabbled in training, security and safety. All the enterprises in which I worked shaped my reality of how people behave, both well and badly, within complex organizations.

I'm now happily retired and consider myself both a survivor and a beneficiary of Corporate America. Though at times I felt the pain born of tough experiences, the rewards, by far, exceeded the tough times. It is also significant to me, having immigrated to this wonderful country, that like millions before me who had nothing when they came, I was able to reap the rewards of working hard and achieving a level of success that I could hardly fathom when I first arrived.

As I wrote this book, I reached out to colleagues I have known through the years and asked them to share their people experiences in Corporate America ranging from the good, to the bad to the plain ugly. Some of their quotes, perspectives and stories are included throughout this book. All of their perspectives were helpful in selecting the topics I cover in the book. All but one are seasoned leaders. I focused on this group because of their years of experience that have made them, in my opinion, tested and proven leaders. The industries they represent include retail, healthcare providers, restaurants, professional associations, manufacturing, information technology consulting, real estate investment trusts, publishing and oil. Their professional backgrounds include finance, marketing, sales, human resources, information technology and, for the most part, operations. I concentrated on operations executives because, in most organizations, they are the closest to the paying customer, thus positioning them at the heart of the enterprise. All the contributors have had successful careers and are role models and mentors to many in the corporate arena.

I have been blessed to work with some of the brightest and most well-balanced people I could wish for, and I have worked with some of the biggest Dumb Asses and Egomaniacs you can imagine. Throughout my career, I tried to understand what makes great people successful. I also tried to understand the Egomaniacs and Dumb Asses that make some corporate environments so challenging. Every company I worked at had its pluses and minuses, and my intent is not to single any one out. Though the cultures were different in each organization, they all had outstanding people along with their fair share of Barbarians.

To thrive in the for-profit capitalist world requires great thinking, strong leadership, inspired vision and a sense of urgency. It also requires resilience, the ability to execute and a strong belief in your product or service. With great leadership comes the challenge of making tough decisions about strategies, resources and people. Nonetheless, there is a right way and a wrong way to be tough. A friend once gave me a plaque that hung in my office for many years. It said, "It is impossible to do the wrong thing right." You must be tough to thrive in the corporate world. You don't, however, have to be a Dumb Ass or an Egomaniac. If you are still curious, welcome. Here is what lies ahead.

The Book

Chapter One is devoted to individual contributor Warriors who do things the right way. Specifically, I'll outline traits that make these Warriors invaluable to their companies.

Chapter Two is devoted to a description of traits typical to Warriors in leadership roles.

Chapter Three focuses on Dumb Asses. This is the first type of Barbarian who can be found in the corporate world. In this chapter, I'll outline traits that make these people such obstacles.

Chapter Four describes Egomaniacs, the second type of Barbarian who roams within the corporate arena.

Chapter Five addresses the importance of mentors and the critical role they play in helping you navigate a world populated by Barbarians.

Chapter Six is devoted to what makes major functional departments in corporations either vital to, or a drag on, the business.

Chapter Seven is devoted to the lunacy that some people (mostly Dumb Asses), functions or corporations create through confusing communications.

Chapter Eight is about the potential people-related maladies that can occur when companies grow too fast.

Chapter Nine focuses on critically important things I learned from both Warriors and Barbarians during my own corporate journey.

Chapter Ten concludes this work with parting perspectives about Warriors and Barbarians and a challenge to the readers.

CHAPTER ONE

The Foundational Traits of Warriors

Hundreds of books have been written about how to succeed at this, be better at that, improve your skills, etc. I believe most skill building is grounded in common sense, but in attempts to spin or be unique, a great deal of what you'll find in books is frightfully confusing. Here is my proposition: People are wired a certain way. A mix of genealogy and the culture you are born into means you are conditioned to be good at something. Can you change course? I believe it's possible, within limits. For example, I love football and would have given anything to be a professional wide receiver. It was not going to happen. I was too slow, my hands were mediocre, and I lacked even a shred of leaping ability. As a result, my reality suggested that I should pursue a different profession. Could consultants, coaches and teachers have helped me to be a better football player? Probably, but I suspect I would still not be good enough.

To dream is great, but to optimize what you are really good at is divine. Yes, it's a struggle for many of us to identify our strengths, but therein lies the first and most important trait of the Warrior.

Warriors cherish the journey of self-discovery. Warriors know how vital it is to define who they are.

There are PhDs who work on the assembly line or pound nails because they love to build. There are doctors who started their education in the fine arts. There are heads of corporations with no degrees or non-business degrees. Does anyone really think Bill Gates would have achieved more had he finished college? Think about what you wanted to be when you were a child, and then fast forward to high school, college or your first job. What were your aspirations then? Seldom, if ever, do most of us end up doing what we dreamed of during our formative years. Warriors don't fret the uncertainty. They embrace it and shape it.

To optimize what you are good at does not in any way suggest that Warriors settle. More importantly, Warriors always strive to be better. Some people hold several jobs in different fields throughout their overall career. Others focus on one area. Though not as common as it used to be, some people spend their entire careers with one or two organizations; others relish working in several organizations.

Mother Theresa and the Dali Lama knew their callings almost from birth and spent their lives refining their exemplary roles. They did not compromise. Others found their calling only after toiling in other roles. Still others had a calling but not the means to follow it until later in life. To illustrate, take a look at these famous Warriors and their surprising backgrounds.

- Thomas Edison, who was literally responsible for lighting the world, sold newspapers and was an industrialist and business manager.[1]

- Abraham Lincoln owned a general store, was a captain in the Illinois militia, a self-taught lawyer, a postmaster and a surveyor. He started his political career by serving in the

Illinois House of Representatives before eventually becoming president.[2]

- Clint Eastwood was a hay bailer, logger, truck driver, steel furnace stoker and in the military before becoming an actor, director, producer and composer.[3]

- The Iron Lady, Margaret Thatcher, was a research chemist and barrister before her political career took off.[4]

- George Washington Carver, one of the most prominent scientists and inventors of his time, was born into slavery. He was accepted to Highland College in Highland, Kansas, but denied admittance once college administrators learned of his race.[5]

- Miguel de Cervantes, author of *Don Quijote,* was a soldier, slave and unsuccessful playwright.[6]

- Amelia Earhart, a trailblazer for women pilots, held jobs as a photographer, social worker, teacher and truck driver to earn money to support her flying lessons.[7]

So is the drive for self-improvement sufficient to be considered a Warrior? In a word: No. In addition to following and cultivating their calling, Warriors also share traits that separate them from the mediocre, people who are happy with just getting by. Much of what differentiates the great from the merely mortal is simply common sense. The problem is that common sense is not as common as we'd like to think. Furthermore, being a Warrior requires dedication. Just because you possess a trait does not mean you practice it. Just because you have a certain skill does not mean you optimize it. Therefore, as you review the following list, put yourself on introspective mode.

As you review these attributes, ask yourself: Am I practicing that skill? Are my behaviors in line with what Warriors do? Better yet, on a regular basis ask those whose judgment you trust how they think you are doing with X skill or Y behavior. We are human. We slip. The challenge is not to master something and move on. The challenge is to sustain and build key skills and behaviors. To do that requires discipline, introspection and perspectives from trusted colleagues, family and friends. You bear the burden of ensuring you are improving your skills and behaviors, but you don't have to do it alone.

Below is a list of what I strongly believe are the primary traits of Warriors.

Warriors are Action Oriented

Warriors take action when it is necessary. They don't fight every battle, because common sense does not make that practical. Be it a task, a project or a critical decision, Warriors get it done. Often they have to get it done because the Dumb Asses are lagging behind or the Egomaniacs are too busy dealing in their currency of self-aggrandizement to get any real work done.

More importantly, Warriors take action for the sake of improvement, for the customer, because it is good for the enterprise and/or because it is the right thing to do. Think of the thousands of interactions that take place in the course of your daily routines in banks, grocery stores, restaurants, doctor's offices, etc. Who do you gravitate to? The doers, the action takers, the people you know will answer your question or help you to find the answer. The people you know will make it right or make it easier.

For those of us who report up to someone at a higher level (that would be everyone below God), we are often dependent on our superiors for critical information. Think about the frustration of needing critical information to proceed with a project or finalize something important but you can't get the input you require from your boss. Does the boss give you what you need every time? Of course not, but Warrior bosses make the decision, give you the support you seek or explain why they can't. When possible they also help you figure out an alternative to address the issue. They take action. Even if they can't help you solve your problem, they don't leave you hanging in the wind. And even though you may not like the answer or the alternative, you won't linger in confusion and frustration.

Warriors Possess a Value-added Mentality

Warriors are not satisfied with simply building the chair, finishing the report, ringing up the order or giving patients their medications. The Warrior mindset is to improve and enhance. Mediocre is failure to the Warrior. They have a personal investment in "better."

Go back to the chair maker or the nurse dispensing medication. They can execute the requisite tasks in their sleep, but without the mindset to make what they do better, their jobs become a series of mundane tasks. Warrior chair makers do not think of building chairs; they think of building thrones. Warrior nurses dispensing medications do not think in terms of checking off another task on the to-do list. Instead, they think about influencing their patients' safety, comfort and happiness and in the process create added value that the medication itself cannot.

Complacency is not in the Warrior's mindset. They need the intrinsic affirmation that what they do is above and beyond what is required or necessary. Is it realistic to do that with every single task? No, but consider the alternative. Going through the motions of just getting things done is boring, debilitating and stifling.

> *"An IT Manager that I worked with had an ability to never leave any problem unresolved. He would work until he figured out what the issue was, sometimes working on several issues simultaneously. Several times the problems did not have anything to do with his job, but because someone asked for his help he would always make sure to lead you*

in the right direction and find the solution. That level of customer service and dedication has always inspired me. Even with technical issues, he never felt the need to speak in 'IT-language' but instead was always focused on making sure you had the resources you needed and that you understood the 'why's' and 'what's' of a situation."

— Erica Navarro, Operations Manager, Colorado Society of Certified Public Accountants

Warriors Are Well-grounded

Warriors know who they are and seek balance in their personal and professional lives. Knowing who they are includes the introspection to know what they are good at and what they need to improve upon. Warriors are not afraid of admitting they don't know something critical, and they take the initiative to learn. They are not afraid to admit that they lack certain skills and seek ways to develop them. They recognize there are countless situations where they "don't know what they don't know," and seek guidance from those who can provide knowledge or perspective. They are not paralyzed by these challenges. They take action to overcome them.

Balance in a Warrior's personal life does not mean that everything is perfect. People experience broken relationships, illnesses, deaths of family or friends, accidents and a myriad of other maladies. In some cases, the person has some ability to control what happens, but in many cases, there is no control at all. The Warriors' perspective allows them to put adversity in its proper place and to keep on moving and growing. They retain the ability to change focus and to ensure that the most important things are being attended to, even if it means taking a step back at work or, harder yet, prioritizing work over their personal life.

Some people are born with an inner strength that allows them to put adversity in its proper place and manage it. Most of us, though, experience life events that help us along the way (see the example of George Washington Carver on page 3).

Think about adversity you lived through and then ask yourself if you gained some perspective from it. How did it help you balance? Some people allow adversity to paralyze them or, in extreme cases, literally destroy them. Some become bitter or want to make life miserable for others.

How many times have you been with, or around, an Egomaniac or Dumb Ass who went on and on about something of little or no value or significance? They love to invest themselves in the misery. They wallow in playing the victim. They lack both grounding and balance. Conversely, how many times have you heard about, or had direct experience with, a person who was diagnosed with a serious or even fatal disease and they handle it with optimism and courage? The difference between these two very different approaches is mindset. Barbarians seek misery. Warriors seek balance.

Warriors Seek and Validate Perspectives

Warriors seek others' perspective for the purpose of learning. They seek perspective not as a matter of dependency but in order to grow. Warriors especially pursue perspective regarding decisions they are expected to make that will impart a material impact on the business. Lots of people seek perspective from others but never grow. The perspective from others does not enhance their ability to make decisions or to be proactive. Worse yet, Dumb Asses in particular seek perspective from others but neither validate nor challenge it. They simply accept it as gospel. Dumb Asses tend to make important decisions in a vacuum without taking different perspectives into account.

Warriors recognize that perspective is just a view of something or an opinion about something and as such can be distorted. Therefore, Warriors will not accept perspective as gospel. They understand that some perspective is tainted or warped. Where possible, Warriors try to validate critical perspectives or, at a minimum, question them. Is the perspective logical given the facts? Is the source of the perspective biased? Could the source, regardless how reliable, have a hidden agenda or ulterior motive?

The degree to which Warriors question perspectives is dependent upon how critical the issue is. Seeking perspective on minor decisions is not perceived as a big deal. Moreover, when the Warrior receives lousy opinions regarding a minor issue and acts on it to his or her detriment, it is not a big deal. Warriors learn from the experience and move on. If the perspective is about a major decision that will affect a large group or has material impact on the enterprise, the Warrior not only questions and validates but when possible seeks multiple perspectives from multiple sources.

Consider any major decision in your enterprise that affected customers or employees across the board. Think of an instance where you were either partly or wholly responsible for the decision. Now flash back to the time before the decision was made and ask yourself if all parties involved had the same perspectives. Of course, they didn't. If that decision resulted in success, did some of the pre-decision doubters change their perspective? If the decision resulted in failure, did the number of pre-decision doubters grow? I'll leave you to your answers. I think I know what they are.

Perspective is a critical component in the fine line between success and failure. The proverbial oncoming train eventually hits those who make major decisions without seeking it. Major decisions made in a vacuum are, at some point, bound to turn out badly.

Warriors Possess Solid Intuition

Achieving professional maturity comes with experience. You don't walk into your first job endowed with professional maturity. Because professional maturity is not inbred, it makes intuition very important.

My definition of intuition in the workplace includes the following:

- **The ability to read people and identify their personal style.**
  Intuition is especially useful for identifying the Barbarians.
  Whether in school, social settings or family events, the ability
  to accurately identify personal styles is invaluable. Who wants
  to hang around with Egomaniacs or Dumb Asses? Conversely,
  don't you want to optimize the time you spend interacting
  with people that you respect and admire? You may not have
  as much choice in the matter in the work setting, but if you
  are stuck with a Barbarian, knowing it early is important to
  managing the relationship.

- **The ability to read people in the moment to identify issues
  lurking beneath the surface**. How many times in your life
  did you unknowingly walk into an uncomfortable or tense
  situation? How many times did you witness this happening
  to others? We all experienced it in one way or another. In the
  workplace it takes on a thousand forms and shapes: The meeting that no one but the boss thinks is necessary; the discussions
  that do not address the underlying or real issues; the trauma
  or personal upheaval that a colleague may be trying to hide;
  the customer that could care less about rationalizations and
  only wants their problem solved; the attempts by someone to
  manipulate solely for their gain, etc.

The ability to accurately read situations like those listed above
is invaluable in deciding what role you should play and what
approach you should take. It is easy in any of these situations
to get frustrated quickly or become a victim of circumstances.
Warriors maintain a sagacious grasp of issues beneath the
surface and adjust their approach to fit the circumstances.

- **The good sense to know when to speak and when to shut up.** How many parties have you been to, family gatherings etc., when you wanted to leap across the room and shove a muzzle on someone who talks and talks for the sake of speaking? Moreover, much of what is coming out of their mouth seems to range from the extremes of the trite to proselytizing. In social or family gatherings you can shut down or walk away; unfortunately, it is not that easy in the workplace, where these types of experiences can be painful. Accordingly, Warriors are respectful when the motor-mouths are in full gear, but they work at getting the situation on track by professionally making suggestions that additional focus is needed. More importantly, Warriors themselves are not verbose. Instead, they are measured and clear in their communication. They have the intuitive trait of knowing their audience and tailoring their message. The Warrior is also content to remain silent if the point has already been made.

The list of attributes to define intuition could arguably be much longer. I included only those traits that, I believe, are most valuable in the workplace. If you don't feel you possess these traits, gravitate toward people who do and learn from them.

Warriors Know How to Disagree Without Being Disagreeable

It's likely you've heard some people described as possessing the ability to tell you that your head is up your butt but do it in a way that lets you walk away feeling good about it. This is a truly rare and valuable skill. Put differently, it is important to attack the issues and not the person.

It is impossible to make a positive impact on your enterprise or colleagues without disagreement. If you are not disagreeing at some point about something critical, you are not applying yourself. Either you are not trying very hard, or you simply don't care.

Disagreement done the right way enriches the debate, the thinking and the perspectives. Disagreement done the right way leads to better outcomes. Much has been written about communications, including the verbal and the non-verbal. It is valuable to know when you are going to disagree and to have a plan to do it the right way. The more important the issue at hand, the more critical is the need to be prepared to disagree if necessary.

Warriors know their audience and the circumstances involved in the issue and, whenever possible, they prepare. They do so by being fact-based, by knowing who is responsible for making the final decisions, by seeking understanding of the counter-point and most importantly, by focusing on moving forward and not simply dwelling on the disagreement. When Warriors do not have time to prepare, they engage disagreement in a thoughtful and measured way, ensuring they hold a good enough grasp of the issues to be convincing but not destructive. Asking clarifying questions about the topic or asking questions that probe about the person's underlying beliefs about the issue are good ways to get a handle on an unexpected confrontation. Sometimes, the only way to successfully manage unpredictable disagreements is to walk away, get the facts and, re-engage when the time is right.

If you are trying to do anything of value and you are true to yourself, you are going to piss some people off. Employing the ability to minimize how angry or annoyed people may be with you is invaluable.

> *"My recollection of a really good co-worker was that he was brutally honest, had a great sense of humor and was a strong advocate to have on your side."*
>
> — KIM BAYER, DIVISION MARKETING OFFICER, MCDONALD'S CORPORATION

Warriors are Solid at Analyzing Situations

Different roles require different levels of analysis. There is a wide spectrum in the degree of analysis required to mow a lawn versus building a rocket. The differentiating factors for the Warrior are first, what needs to be analyzed and second, to what degree. You are likely familiar with the phrase "paralysis by analysis." At some point analysis needs to convert into decisions or actions. Regardless of their role, Warriors recognize when analysis is morphing into paralysis. The Dumb Asses are good at the paralysis stuff; they thrive on it. More than once in my career, I wish I could have invoked "Occam's razor" upon the procrastinators. "Occam's razor" is a theorem that suggests that the simplest answer is most often correct.[8] That is not always going to be the case, but, for the procrastinators, it is certainly a better alternative than needless delay.

Analysis can take many forms. It may include data, gathering opinions, or testing. The Warrior is comfortable with all types, including the ability to reframe issues and to analyze them from a different place or an alternate mindset. Warriors can tear down the artificial barriers, restraints or parameters that tend to be placed around things, people or issues.

Warriors recognize the need for thoughtful and measured analysis. They devote the appropriate time to analyze and give their findings the proper weight and convert the results into decisions and actions. They recognize that analysis alone amounts to nothing if it does not lead to adding value. Analysis may, at times, lead to a decision not to proceed or to take a different path. In any case, analysis requires closure.

Warriors Are Persistent and Resilient

Often times getting things done is more about persistence than anything else. A great idea at the wrong time turns quickly into a bad idea. A great idea without the proper support is destined for the trash heap. A great idea without the proper execution will fail. Thus, for some ideas to come to fruition and turn into something tangible, persistence is required.

Sometimes persistence means pushing the issue until you get the proper support to get it done. It means taking a breath and putting the issue off to the side until the climate is better for it to come to fruition. Sometimes it is gutting it out through trial and error without losing faith that what you are doing is worth the pain. At times, holding the course can lead to generating significant value. Sometimes it's going back to something that failed but now has the opportunity to succeed. We have all heard the line, "We tried that before, and it didn't work." That may be true but perhaps it didn't work because of timing or just possibly because Barbarians were at the helm. It takes courage, commitment and belief in something to make it work. Warriors recognize that, at times, the most critical weapon in the arsenal is persistence. The late, great football coach Vince Lombardi put it in perspective: "Once you learn to quit, it becomes a habit."[9]

A dimension of persistence is resilience. Being resilient in the corporate world is a must if you are to achieve any degree of success. The barriers, setbacks and challenges of keeping enterprises competitive and growing can be daunting. In the restaurant world, labor and food costs are literally measured by the hour. The manager checks it to manage it on a daily basis, as does the manager's boss, as does the boss's boss. In manufacturing, inventory, productivity and getting product out the door are measured and re-measured. The pressures of these daily activities alone require strong resiliency. Layer on top of that the unexpected pressures, the need to innovate, to stay current with new processes and products, and resiliency becomes all that more important. Anything new usually means change and learning. A dear friend and colleague used to tell me all the time that "staying number one required changing the tires on the car while it was still moving." Warriors understand and embrace that concept.

Warriors Love to Be Measured and Held Accountable

Corporations are all about the numbers. Though some numbers (e.g., sales trends, operating income, return on assets, return on investment, etc.) get a lot of attention, just about everything that goes on in the enterprise gets measured to some degree. People who hide from measurement are inevitably doomed to be the victims of poor results.

Measurement shows whether you are growing or shrinking, improving or regressing. Front-line operations take care of the paying customer and make the money, but if you are in a support role and not measuring how you impact the enterprise, you are not integral to the business. You are irrelevant, and, worse yet, you are a burden.

Having worked in a support function (or overhead), I always talked to subordinates and colleagues about the concept of value-added. Specifically, I challenged people in support roles to pretend they did not receive a regular check from the company. I asked them to instead think of themselves as independent consultants: if their contributions to the company were not perceived as value-added, then they would not get any more business (which translated as paychecks).

With measurement comes accountability. Simply said, you are responsible and accountable for your results. Accountability is not solely about measurement. There is accountability for getting things done. If you manage people, you are also accountable for the actions and results of your direct reports. And if you are a member of a team, you are accountable for anything requiring cross-functional collaboration. Some folks are accountable to multiple bosses (always fun). But if that is the job, Warriors accept it.

Warriors embrace accountability and are the first to step up when they have made a mistake or failed to achieve a key milestone. They admit it openly, take ownership of it, fix what needs fixing and move on. Conversely, when Warriors experience significant success, they share the credit.

Warriors Challenge the Status Quo

Challenging the status quo is paramount if enterprises wish to stay vibrant. There are companies that have gotten themselves in trouble, if not ceased to exist, primarily because they became complacent. They may have had a great product or business model and stuck with it beyond its expected life span. The same thing can happen in functional departments within the enterprise. Some departments develop a way to do things, or a certain culture, and when the needs of the enterprise change, they resist it. This is a precursor to failure.

Warriors know that by challenging the status quo they are forcing themselves and those they impact to stay current and relevant to the needs of the enterprise. Change is not an option in business; change is a guaranteed part of doing business. Accordingly, Warriors are comfortable with change. It has been said that people, for the most part, are not uncomfortable with change; rather, they are uncomfortable with change being thrust on them. The Warriors challenge the status quo and by doing so shape and manage the changes necessary for the enterprise to remain vibrant.

> *"One of the reasons that managers have gotten to the place they landed in the organization is that they obey the status quo. Never forget that there is a time for disobedience. My bosses who have been 'managers' have looked at innovation as a distraction. What they don't account for is the velocity of change in the marketplace today. Today, and in the near future, generations are being defined in six-year increments versus the 15 to 20 year increments of the generations they are more familiar with. They avoid risks because they look at such actions as disobedience.*

> *"Effective leaders understand that leading is more about managing risks versus being risk-averse. Put in the boundary*

that ensures execution of the core elements of your plan,
but always leave room for innovation; this is a pipeline for
your future."

— MIKE ANDRES, CHAIRMAN AND CHIEF EXECUTIVE
OFFICER, LOGAN'S ROADHOUSE INC.

Warriors Execute Their Roles in the Context of the Greater Enterprise

The larger the enterprise, the more subject matter experts there will be in the organization. Whether they work on the shop floor or in the offices, people will perform a specific function, sometimes very narrow in scope that supports some part of the greater enterprise. It is easy for those who work in these roles to get into the "silo mentality," thinking that what they do is valued by everyone or that what they do is more important than what others do. Worse yet is the belief that everyone understands what they do.

Regardless of their roles, Warriors do their work based on the understanding that they are part of a much larger whole. They do not take anyone for granted or lapse into the silo mentality. Folks in staff roles also appreciate that their work impacts the people on the front line (the people who interact with the customer). Accordingly, anything the staff person can do to make things simple is value-added. The front-line person is impacted in some way, at some time, by all the support functions. Accordingly, front-line people appreciate what is simple to understand and simple to execute. Simple is also great for the customer. A staff person who designs anything that touches the customer should strive for this focus: simple to buy, to use and to service.

The silo mentality causes staff people to lose sight of their roles and their importance. They forget that they exist to support the front-line and instead become a burden. One of the biggest frustrations of the front-line person is to divert from taking care of the paying customer to deal with requests from staff. These are especially frustrating if the requests are perceived as bureaucratic or overly cumbersome. Some bureaucracy is unavoidable, but bureaucracy for its own sake is an abysmal waste of time and resources. Conversely, the front-line Warriors recognize that staff functions do not exist solely for support. For example, they appreciate that some staff functions have fiduciary responsibilities that require attention.

Warriors Love to Learn

Learning is critical to the value that Warriors place on professional growth. Warriors use their resources but also want to be as self-sufficient and self-reliant as possible. Seeking knowledge to improve their effectiveness, they want to know more about their current area of expertise, their overall enterprise and their industry.

The learning experts contend that different people use various ways of learning. Some people need to do things and be hands-on to learn. The preferred method of others is reading or observing. Some may need a combination. Whatever learning style you prefer is okay. That said, there is no teacher like experience. Accordingly, there is no better learning opportunity than experience.

Each year, literally billions of dollars are spent on skill-building workshops and seminars on every topic imaginable. Some have value. But it has never ceased to amaze me how many of these I attended that were so superficial I considered them a waste of time and money. In my experience, technical topics or more focused offerings tend to be more valuable than those that are broad in nature. I found that Soft Skill and leadership seminars tend to repackage the same principles over and over. Even among the better workshops/seminars, the value is not necessarily in the content; rather, the value is found in the interactions with the other attendees, specifically learning from each other's experiences and building relationships. This is not an indictment on seminars and workshops. It will serve you well to keep in mind that attending these events is an investment of time and money. Before committing to attend one of these learning sessions, you should do your homework. Specifically, the following questions should be answered:

- Is the event accredited by your professional organization?
- Does the Better Business Bureau list reviews on the seminar?
- Has someone whose judgment you trust attended, and do they recommend it?
- Who attends the seminar? Check what companies are represented and the position level of the attendees. Are these companies you admire, and are the attendees people you'd like to meet?

Finally, if you are in a leadership role and a direct report is attending a workshop, you should ensure that the person is prepared to report on what was learned and how that employee plans to apply this newly acquired information in his or her job. Where applicable, have the attendee report the same to peers and other leadership.

As a leader, I always valued the Warriors who volunteered or requested to conduct research on some important issue or to be on a special assignment or team. Cross-functional teams are especially valuable in that each team member gets the opportunity to spend time with staff they may not interact with on a regular basis. I could not always accommodate requests by my subordinates to be part of a special assignment, but I certainly took note and looked for opportunities for that individual to expand beyond their role. Warriors take the initiative to be part of something important and to learn.

"Many authors have tried to define and categorize leadership and the qualities of productive people, some more realistically than others. I have found the formal training I received to be helpful throughout the years, but there is no substitute for experience and the informal ideas and concepts that my career afforded me. I am reminded of the critical nature

of this informal process as I reflect on my good fortune to work with an Ivy League PhD candidate while leading the third-largest territory in the company.

"Her thesis revolved around the theory that informal training was far more important to the success of the individual, thus the organization, and far more than the formal training on which companies spend millions of dollars on an annual basis. This theory cut across all disciplines and concepts, including leadership training. She worked with five companies from five major industry groups. We are all a collection of numerous planned and unplanned events and situations, most that you could never anticipate or experience in a formal way. This collection is comprised of positive, tough and invaluable learning experiences."

— DAVE DANIELS, OWNER DOUBLE D CONSULTING AND FORMER VP OF OPERATIONS, SPORT CLIPS, INC.

Warriors Have a Sense of Urgency and Honor Their Commitments

Warriors strongly believe that what they do, and what they contribute to the enterprise, is important. As such, they do it with a sense of urgency. A key component of working with a sense of urgency is keeping commitments. Of course, not every commitment can be kept. When that happens, Warriors follow up with stakeholders to communicate that the commitment cannot be met, explains why, and, if applicable, has a plan B. If there is no plan B, the Warrior apologizes and accepts responsibility.

Think about the following: You are dependent on a co-worker to finish a project or take care of a customer. Your co-worker commits but does not deliver. More likely than not, the repeat offenders who do not live up to their commitments are the Dumb Asses. Avoid them when practical, but, if need be, confront them and let them know that their lackadaisical ways are hurting the enterprise. Be specific and focus on behaviors, facts and outcomes. Don't attack the person. Instead, attack the problems they produce. It may not do any good in terms of getting the Dumb Ass to act differently, but it sets the stage to take the issue to a higher level if necessary. One of my golden rules was to not talk about a peer's failings to a superior unless I talked to that peer first. Once you have done that, you should feel comfortable elevating the issues that are detrimental to the enterprise even if it involves others.

Working with a sense of urgency sends a message to colleagues that you are responsible and are driven to get things done. It also sends a message that you are about what is best for the organization, including confronting the Barbarians when necessary.

Warriors Are Driven to Be the Best but Not at the Expense of the Enterprise or Co-workers

Whether for personal or other reasons, some Warriors are not career-oriented. They are satisfied with where they are at and strive to be the best at what they do. Moreover, they help others along the way because they know it is the right thing to do for the co-worker and for the enterprise. Have you ever been in a situation where you were the new person on a team or department and the person responsible for your orientation and/or training did everything possible to make your life miserable? Warriors do their best to ensure people new to the team receive the orientation and training needed to succeed. It is not just about new co-workers. Warriors will help tenured coworkers if they are struggling with a new process, tool or program.

However, many Warriors are career-oriented and recognize that moving up in organizations requires more than just solid performance. Being noticed by leadership requires some level of self-marketing. As an example, opportunities to serve on ad-hoc or formal teams or other activities can raise your profile. But if those opportunities are not managed correctly, such activities can be perceived as self-serving or done at the expense of others. It is, therefore, important to ensure that when success is achieved, appropriate credit is given to all who contributed. And when opportunities arise to serve on teams or special projects, your participation should be done in the spirit of collaboration and not by assuming that you are the best choice for the assignment.

At times being noticed as an upwardly mobile person may involve doing things that are good for the enterprise but not necessarily the individual. For example, the timing of a capital investment and the corresponding impact on financial statements, investing in labor to stabilize a high-turnover situation or ensuring that people are trained may adversely impact costs in the short run. Warriors are conscious of these developments and ensure that the actions they take to prepare themselves for promotion are thoughtful and consistent with what is right for co-workers and the enterprise.

About the List

Arguably, the list of the key Warrior attributes is long. It is easy to say there are too many things to work on and too many things to refine. I submit this: there is nothing on the list that is extraordinary or special in any way. There are attributes on the list you are already good at and others that you may have to strengthen and refine. If you agree that the traits above are important, then it is as simple as saying, "I agree that these attributes are important and commit to refining each one." Part of this process is being honest with yourself and being introspective about what you need to work on. It is also important to ask for input from colleagues or superiors who know you and whose judgment you trust. You should make it comfortable for people to give you input on your skills, on your work product and how you are perceived.

As Warriors strengthen these traits, they gain confidence in themselves, their professional style and their comfort in navigating the Barbarian-infested waters of the corporate world. Just as importantly, they make the enterprise better and invariably become role models to others.

Confidence, not arrogance, is a strong force. It helps people to act with conviction and purpose to succeed and to win. One of the most common beliefs regarding competition, whether in sports, school, warfare or the corporate world, is if you play not to lose, that will be the most likely outcome. Confidence also provides the individual with the strength to lose but to do so with dignity and purpose. To get knocked down and get back up and try again is born of confidence that, at the very least, you tried and you learned from the failure.

Finally, confidence helps Warriors to overcome lousy leadership or direction. At some point, most of us will work for a Barbarian. Some of us have worked for one more than once. Valuing and improving the skills and behaviors covered in this chapter builds confidence and will help Warriors to navigate around crappy leadership.

> *"The best co-workers are team-players, selfless, think big picture and never put themselves first."*
> — JOHN DECARRIER, MCDONALD'S FRANCHISEE

> *"The best co-workers I had were not competitive with other workers. They wanted what was best for the company, were people champions who wanted everyone to succeed, held others accountable and were not afraid to stand up for what is right."*
> — VICKI GUSTER-HINES, REGIONAL VICE PRESIDENT OF OPERATIONS, MCDONALD'S CORPORATION

A Note to Leaders Seeking Warriors

If you are searching for people for your department or team within your enterprise, I believe the very best predictor of Warrior behaviors is observation. If you don't know the person, ask those you trust for a perspective. Use the list of attributes as your guide regarding what questions to ask about the person. Results and history of accomplishments are important, but of and by themselves they can be misleading. People can be part of a team that is very successful, but they themselves contributed little, if anything, to the success. People can be at the right place at the right time and benefit from it without contributing. Conversely, I recall throughout my career many examples of people who performed admirably but suffered from being at the wrong place at the wrong time in a business cycle or because of circumstances beyond their control.

If practical, spend time with an individual and get to know how she thinks and conducts herself. I'm not suggesting an interview as I assume that will happen somewhere in the process. I'm talking about focused, one-on-one time with a person. Way too much emphasis is placed on interviews at the expense of trying to know the person beyond their ability to articulate answers to interview questions.

.References are important if you are looking for people from outside the enterprise, but if you don't know the person providing the reference, the information you obtain can be misleading. A way to get more direct insight is to invite the candidate to spend a day at your enterprise and have them interact with as many potential team members as possible and also with your customers.

If you are hiring someone into a managerial role and the person has leadership experience, try to get perspectives from people who reported to the individual. Also ask the candidate to spend time with the people they will lead and solicit perspectives from those people.

Regarding interviews, there are literally hundreds of insightful questions you can ask. There are web sites where you can find potential questions, and most enterprises provide formal interview protocols that include questions tied to competencies, leadership traits, etc. To the extent that it is possible, I believe in asking questions that provide insight about how the candidate thinks and what they have learned from their experiences. It is also important to try to gain insight into who the person is, how professional they are, and what life experiences shaped them. These insights are not things that you are likely to see on a resume.

Psychological and intelligence tests have become more and more popular. Most of these are done with the understanding that they are intended to help the individual being evaluated with their professional development. In most cases, that is what happens. Unfortunately, I have also experienced situations where these tests were used as a reason not to promote someone, sometimes in spite of a great track record of results and consistent demonstration of Warrior skills. Just as an interview alone should not be used as the sole basis for a hiring or promotion decision, psychological/intelligence tests should not be the sole basis for these decisions.

One final note regarding the selection of Warriors: Ensure, as a leader, that you know who is making the hiring and promotion decisions in your organization. Even more crucial is your comfort level that these people can be trusted with those responsibilities. At its crudest and most irreverent, you don't want Dumb Asses and Egomaniacs making hiring and promotion decisions. The former will select people at or below their low level of competence, and the latter will select people in their own image or, worse yet, people who will feed their egos.

One of my more memorable experiences was trying to literally upgrade the leadership of our operations group from the unit level up through the senior levels. After analyzing the challenge, the Chief Operating Officer and I made the decision that we had to restrict who was making hiring and promotion decisions. As the COO put it, "On a scale of one to ten (ten being the best), we have fives making hiring and promotion decisions, and we need eights or better to make a long-term impact on the organization." The fives could not recognize an eight or better if they bit them. Either that or the fives were threatened by the higher-caliber candidates and so settled for much less. This is not a good position in which to find yourself if you are trying to upgrade talent at any level.

Navigating the Mishmash of Bad Advice

Several times throughout my career, I was responsible for a large staff of people. One position I inherited involved more than 30 staff. I knew a handful of them, but most I had never met. I had also inherited two direct reports upon whom I had to initially rely for input regarding the skill level of these people. I knew one of my direct reports from having worked with her earlier and, at best, I thought she was not in a role that suited her skill set. That her role had influence in the development of other people concerned me. I did not know the second direct report, but my early vibes about him were not positive. I asked both for input on all the staff, knowing full well that I could not trust the input without direct calibration and/ or relying on others for perspective.

Regarding one person in particular, the input I received from my two direct reports was so egregiously inconsistent with the input I received from other people I trusted that I made it a priority to visit with the individual to get my own direct read. My two direct reports had painted a picture of an individual who should not be in Human Resources, was not growing professionally and had no future with the company. After personally visiting with this person, I was so impressed with her that I not only committed to helping her in any way I could but also wanted to ensure I provided opportunities for her to grow beyond her role at the time. Long story short, I had to deal with my two direct reports, and the person they thought to be so lousy turned out to be one of the best examples of a true Warrior that I ever had the privilege to know. She was promoted three times in four years and is widely recognized as having the potential to continue to ascend to higher-level leadership roles within the organization. Sometimes Dumb Asses can be very helpful if you do the opposite of what they recommend.

CHAPTER SUMMARY

Warriors:

- *Are action oriented*
- *Possess a value-added mentality*
- *Are well-grounded*
- *Seek and validate perspectives*
- *Possess solid intuition*
- *Know how to disagree without being disagreeable*
- *Are solid at analyzing situations*
- *Are persistent and resilient*
- *Love to be measured and held accountable*
- *Challenge the status quo*
- *Execute their roles in the context of the greater enterprise*
- *Love to learn*
- *Have a sense of urgency and keep their commitments*
- *Are driven to be the best but not at the expense of the enterprise or co-workers*

CHAPTER TWO

The Traits of Warriors in Leadership Roles

To be a true Warrior Leader, you must already possess all of the foundational traits covered in Chapter One. Accordingly, the traits of Warrior Leaders are those that are primarily associated with the profound responsibility of guiding a major area or department of the enterprise or the company itself.

Warrior Leaders Keep Their Egos in Check

Make no mistake; it takes a healthy ego to succeed in leadership positions in corporations—but to let the whole world see it and feel it is not in the mix for Warrior Leaders. Take, for example, Amy Wambach of the US Women's National Soccer Team. The lady has unbelievable talent and is a tremendous leader with an incredible resume. She has plenty to brag about but does not. Her ego seems to always be in the proper place, which is on the soccer field doing what she does best. When her teammates make mistakes, she does not berate them. Instead, she encourages them. When she does something great, she uses it as a means to encourage her team to do better. Warrior Leaders in corporations are the same. They have lots of ego to take issues and people head-on, but they focus on the challenge at hand instead of letting their ego show like a peacock with its feathers raised.

Keeping the ego in check goes hand-in-hand with Warrior Leaders not taking themselves very seriously. It is a sad but undeniable consequence that, the more seriously people take themselves, the less seriously they are taken by those around them. There was an era when job titles or age went a long ways toward getting people to be taken seriously. In today's work environment, that is not the case. Title, seniority or age may get you some initial respect, but to be respected long-term and to be taken seriously requires reaffirmation of great leadership on a regular basis. Warrior Leaders conduct themselves in a way that makes it clear to all that they take the business and the customer very seriously. At the same time, they do not take themselves seriously. They can laugh at themselves. They are genuine.

Above all, Warrior Leaders treat people at all levels with dignity and respect and are comfortable interacting with people at every level of the organization. They especially value interacting with entry-level workers because they are the ones who do the heavy lifting in most organizations. The Warrior Leader also knows that it is execution at the front line that makes or breaks strategies. They put their egos in check in order to listen to the input, both good and bad, that the front-line people contribute. This is especially important if the input is critical of strategies or tactics that have been developed, and/or blessed, by the Warrior Leader.

Warrior Leaders Value Other Leaders but Are Not Overly Deferential to Them

Senior Leaders who are responsible for other high-level leaders sometimes walk a fine line between allowing them to do their job and showing so much deference that it harms the business. Being respectful of other leaders' judgment is a great trait as long as it does not become a blind spot. Accordingly, the Warrior Leader ensures that:

- There is clarity about the vision of where the business needs to go
- There is clarity about strategies that support the vision
- They calibrate that subordinate leaders have the skill set and/ or resources to get the job done
- They get out of the way and let people do their jobs

That said, the Warrior Leader keeps informed about progress or obstacles. Sometimes the biggest obstacle is the Warrior Leader's direct report. When that is the case, the Warrior Leader sets clear expectations about what needs to change or makes the tough decision to replace the individual.

Too many times I was part of organizations that suffered because top management showed too much deference to a key leader who clearly did not have a handle on what needed to be done or, worse, worked at cross purposes from where the business needed to go. When these situations occur, it is painful for everyone involved, especially the front-line players who have to execute the decisions. It is frustrating and discouraging for people to work under a leader who is primarily in the role because top management is showing deference due to their job title or years with the organization.

At times Boards of Directors suffer from the paralysis of deference. How many times have you read stories about companies that are struggling or in the midst of a major crisis and the CEO or other key leaders are just not performing? Even worse are situations where the CEO and/or other top leaders are acting with total disregard for the business. Do you think it took longer than necessary for the Board of Directors at British Petroleum to replace Tony Hayward as CEO? Among the poor decisions made by Hayward was attending a yachting regatta in the middle of the oil-spill crisis while small-business people all over the Gulf of Mexico were facing uncertainty about their businesses, including the possibility of bankruptcy.[1,2]

If Mr. Hayward did not get your attention, how about Richard Fuld, the head of Lehman Brothers, who steered the company into bankruptcy in 2008? Fuld earned hundreds of millions during the eight years leading up to the debacle, eight years in which he made, blessed or, at the very least, was at the helm when many of the decisions that contributed to the bankruptcy were made.[3] If you are not yet convinced, let me try three more: Andrew Fastow, Kenneth Lay and Jeffrey Skilling. You may remember them from the collapse of Enron.[4, 5] These three executives hurt loyal employees with the loss of their jobs and the decimation of their retirement plans. They also hurt the shareholders and managed to take down Arthur Andersen,[6] at the time one of the largest audit and accountancy firms in the world.

These examples were egregious situations that impacted the respective companies in very profound ways. The same dynamics can be at work within functional departments. Too much deference to leaders by other leaders can be harmful, if not disastrous. Warrior Leaders respect other leaders by letting them do their jobs. However, they calibrate regularly and make adjustments as necessary to ensure the overall well-being of the enterprise.

> *"My long-time boss regularly gave those reporting to him a lot of rope to manage and lead in their areas of responsibility. There was no looking over the shoulder. On the other hand, everyone knew they would be held accountable for their actions along their length of the rope. I was rarely surprised by his response to actions I had to take (prior to any direct discussion with him on a particular issue). This was due to the fact that my boss very clearly communicated, throughout the organization, the values and in-practice behaviors the organization was to honor in all that we did."*
>
> — CHARLES G. ZEISSER, FORMER VP OF HUMAN RESOURCES, SSM HEALTHCARE OF WISCONSIN

Warrior Leaders Understand That Most People Need to Be Led but Do not Abuse the Privilege

History is replete with examples of masses of people and entire nations that followed a leader's vision. Some are good, while some are confounding; World War II offers clear examples of both. On the good side, you have Franklin Roosevelt and Winston Churchill. On the confounding side you have Hitler, Mussolini and the Japanese military elite.

Though America was clearly divided about entering the war before Pearl Harbor, the country came together under Roosevelt's leadership to not only enter the war but also to take a lead role with our allies. Churchill was, in my opinion, the "true north" of the allied effort. Long before America entered the war, he rallied the people of his country to fight on against great odds. His vision, resolve and steadfast commitment to not give in to the Nazis and Fascists inspired a nation and the world. Two of his quotes from speeches early in the war say it all:

- **On June 4, 1940 at the House of Commons:** "We shall not flag or fail. We shall go on to the end…We shall fight on the seas and oceans, we shall fight on the beaches, we shall fight on the landing grounds, we shall fight in the fields and in the streets, we shall fight in the hills; we shall never surrender."[7]

- **On June 18, 1940 (after the Battle and Rescue at Dunkirk) at the House of Commons:** "Let us therefore brace ourselves to our duty and so bear ourselves that if the British Empire and its Commonwealth last for a thousand years, men will still say, this was our finest hour."[8]

I'm sure Hitler also had some memorable quotes, but I don't think they deserve to be repeated. What amazes me, though, is not the man but how so many people this murdering psychopath could take in. Viewing tapes of speeches by Hitler is a scary experience, at best. The man looks as if he is the devil incarnate foaming at the mouth. Yet millions followed his leadership at the cost of millions of lives and the obliteration of Germany. Why? Most people need a vision; they need something to believe in and someone to lead the way. This is true for some even when the vision warps into a tragic and unspeakable perversion like Hitler's. This type of blind loyalty happens every day in all walks of life, including the corporate world.

Warrior Leaders lead from the premise that leadership:

- Requires moral courage
- For leadership's sake is just an ego trip, often with humbling consequences
- Factors into the equation the impact that key strategies have on customers, employees and other key stakeholders
- Without guiding values is not focused on the right things and has no direction
- Cannot take the people in an organization for granted, for it is people who will ultimately shape the destiny of the enterprise

"Traits I look for and appreciate in a great leader are:
- *Proactive communicator*
- *Good at being specific about what he/she needs from me and the parameters of my role. They then give me the autonomy to do the job.*
- *Someone who is interested in my development and opinions*
- *Someone who is inclusive*
- *Someone who knows you're a partner in their overall success*
- *Someone who goes beyond the business and makes a connection with me personally*

- *Dependable—keeps commitments and can be trusted—follows through*
- *Someone who can clearly articulate their value structure and walk the walk"*

— WILLIAM J. MCKERNAN, REGIONAL VICE PRESIDENT OF OPERATIONS, MCDONALD'S CORPORATION

Warrior Leaders Are Charismatic, not Flamboyant, Communicators

Lots of people are mesmerized and taken in by people who are flamboyant. Specifically, there are people who get caught up with the glitz without regard to whether the person has any depth, substance or character. Unfortunately we see this phenomenon everywhere in our society.

Warrior Leaders recognize that to be effective they need people who are committed to, and enthusiastic about, the strategies of a department or the company. Accordingly, Warrior Leaders are clear and compelling in their communications and demonstrate a level of excitement that motivates people to act in support of the strategies. Clear and compelling does not mean over-the-top oratory or showiness. It does mean that they communicate in a way that:

- Demonstrates conviction, passion and confidence about the strategies
- Conveys seriousness about the strategies but not themselves
- Includes a sense of humor
- Is straightforward about challenges and obstacles
- Recognizes success as well as failures
- Projects their genuine personality

"The best bosses I've had were the ones who showed they valued you as a person and the skills you brought to the organization. They were able to be humble and self-effacing.

Moreover, they demanded excellence and inspired it. It is a joy working for leaders like that because you know you can make a difference. Finally, my best bosses were trustworthy and not afraid to 'put the duck on the table.' They were not shy about discussing the tough issues no matter how grave. They are clear about the mission and the goals. Bosses who have these traits engender great business results through empowered teams."

— DAVE THOMAS, FORMER CO-PRINCIPAL
AND OFFICER, LCA VISION

Many people may like to be led but not to be deceived or taken for granted. Eventually, most people can see through flamboyancy if a leader has no depth, conviction or substance. Most people eventually figure out when they've been deceived. Unfortunately, regarding the latter, at times realization does not occur until after much harm has been done. How many leaders have you known who are great in front of a group but the more you get to know about them, the less you like or respect them? Most flamboyant leaders, in my experience, are more interested in looking good and being treated like celebrities than they are about doing good.

If you have not been close enough to get to know top leaders, I offer you many of today's politicians by way of example. Many of them are gifted orators but have no substance. They can deliver a speech that will pump you up and leave you crying or screaming for joy. Then they go back to their legislative responsibilities, and nothing gets done. Worse yet, they pass dumb-ass legislation that no one asked for.

Many politicians are in office with the primary goal of being re-elected. How many times have you heard that if companies were run like Congress, the Senate and, for that matter, many government agencies, they would all go bankrupt?

Warrior Leaders know that for the enterprise to thrive and prosper, a combination of great strategies and people committed to great execution is required. The best ideas and strategies are meaningless if people don't embrace them and execute the tactics that support them. Anything can be made to look good on paper, Power Point or "The Dancing Bear" presentation, but if people don't commit, there is nothing. Warrior Leaders are practical, thoughtful and meaningful but not loquacious.

> *"The best bosses I have known were direct, confident, honest, inspiring, caring and compassionate. They empowered their people and rewarded and recognized achievement"*
>
> — Kim Bayer, Division Marketing Officer, McDonald's Corporation

> *"When I think of the best bosses throughout my career, the common traits that I valued about them were honesty, integrity, transparency and the ability to motivate and lead a team."*
>
> — Alma Anguiano, Director, Accelerated Operations Trainee, McDonald's Corporation

Warrior Leaders Keep People Informed About the Things That Matter

Some people expect to be informed 24/7 about everything that is going on in their organization. Some expect to be the first to hear all-important information about what is going on. Both of those expectations are unrealistic and naive. The pace of business, the need to keep certain things confidential and the impact that badly timed information can have on products or the stock price make the timing and content of what is communicated to whom and when very sensitive. There are also regulatory requirements that dictate when some financial information can be reported. Yet all this information doesn't keep the Barbarians from complaining about being the last to know.

At times a department or company may be going through change or unusually heightened activity. During times like these it is important to ensure that there is clear and regular communication between top leaders and the people impacted. In the absence of information, some people will create their own. Inaccurate information is not conducive to keeping people focused. Letting inaccurate information grow can be confusing, if not destructive. There are people that thrive on rumor-mongering and invest themselves in stirring things up. Warrior Leaders do not over-react to accommodate these people, but they do recognize the potentially adverse impact their actions may have on the organization.

Warrior Leaders recognize that people want to know about important developments that impact their positions or the company. Accordingly, Warrior Leaders regularly think in terms of what needs to be communicated to whom, when and how. There is information that is appropriate to communicate via voice-mails or emails, while other communication requires a face-to-face meeting or a one-on-one forum. There are no pat answers to choose the timing and method of communications to all people at all times. Thoughtful consideration of what is important and calibrating with people on a regular basis are common-sense guidelines that Warrior Leaders use to guide them. Above all, Warrior Leaders understand that the more important the issue, the bigger the need to tell people how they will be impacted by it. This is especially important when the news is bad, for example, a downturn in business or a reduction in budgets that may lead to layoffs. Warrior Leaders know that with important issues, they must answer the key question in most employees' minds: "How does this affect me?"

Warrior Leaders Are Great Listeners

Listening is one of the most under-rated yet most meaningful things that leaders need do to be successful. The great listeners focus on what is being said, how it's being said, the context in which it is being said and who is saying it. They listen to learn and truly grasp what is being said. The more important the issue, the more the Warrior Leader listens and the more they seek different and, if need be, conflicting perspectives. It is impossible to learn or understand anything if your lips are in full flapping mode.

Effective listening techniques include:

- Focusing and avoiding distractions
- Paraphrasing for understanding
- Keeping an open mind
- Maintaining good eye contact

All are important and worthy of being mastered, but my point here goes beyond the techniques of effective listening. Rather, it is about the belief that, to be an effective leader, listening has to be a high priority. I'm referring specifically to listening to employees at all levels, to customers and to suppliers. As, if not more, important than listening, is the ability to put what you hear into perspective. The fact that one employee or one customer is irate about something does not necessarily make it a major issue. How often has your boss hauled you into his office about something he heard from a single source and made it sound as if it were an epidemic? Moreover, the source may be unreliable. This is not to suggest that a single source of input is not important, but you have to consider the source and, if need be, validate the input.

The reverse may also be a concern, for example, when the input of an individual is ignored because the person is not popular or may even be a malcontent. The Human Resources department is often the last contact an employee has before leaving the organization. Often, employees take this opportunity to raise serious issues about someone or something with the potential to harm the brand. I have been involved in scenarios like this, and, in many cases, the response from my peers or co-leaders was to ignore the input since it came from a questionable source. The wiser position is to listen. What is the harm? When you hear about something that is troubling, you should not conduct the witch hunts that many of the malcontents would want you to do. Instead, you should sufficiently calibrate to determine if the issues raised have any basis whatsoever. Many companies have initiated whistleblower policies that encourage employees to confidentially raise concerns about potentially illegal or immoral activities. Some have ethics departments that, in part, exist to investigate allegations made by whistleblowers. These are good types of interventions but should not replace the leader's focus on listening and acting on things that deserve attention.

Warrior Leaders Are Decisive and Courageous About Addressing the Tough Issues

The corporate world is not the place to be if you are afraid to make decisions, take too long to deliberate or avoid making decisions. Leaders literally make decisions around the clock; that is the nature of the job. Many decisions are routine, and many have minimal impact. For the purpose of this discussion, let's focus on the tough decisions, the ones that are characterized by uncertainty, high risk or are personally gut-wrenching. Examples include: changing key strategies, terminating a long-term employee or a key leader, laying off numerous people, eliminating a product or investing significant amounts of money.

Tough decisions often require a leader who is comfortable with the uncomfortable. Firing someone, no matter how well deserved, is not easy, and it is not comfortable, but the Warrior Leader makes the decision because it needs to be made. The decision to invest large amounts of the company's capital on a new facility or product can be very uncomfortable unless the investment is all but guaranteed to result in an acceptable return. There are, unfortunately, very few things that are guaranteed, so the leader needs to have the courage to make decisions in the face of varying levels of uncertainty. Oftentimes, the degree of uncertainty can be very high.

Data, the opinions and recommendations of the subject matter experts, the economy, the ability of people to execute, government regulation, environmental issues, time constraints and other factors can be at work when making any given decision. Regarding issues that will broadly impact people in the organization, Warrior Leaders do not rely solely on subject matter experts. They also stay close to, and get perspective from, those who will be affected. In short, they are inclusive where appropriate but not paralyzed by the number of sources of input or by conflicting perspectives.

Leaders who are overly cautious or risk-averse can easily fall into the paralysis-by-analysis mode. Oftentimes, the tougher the decision, the more disagreement exists among the subject matter experts. Marketing wants to do X, but Finance does not support it. Human Resources is recommending the person be fired but Legal is not supportive and on and on. The Warrior Leader relies on past experience, if applicable, along with the facts and their best judgment about what they believe is the right thing to do. The latter should be largely guided by the values of the organization. Values alone won't make the decision easy but they should provide guidance especially in the face of uncertainty. Values also provide an internal check-and-balance that can be helpful in changing the trajectory of a decision, if the person making the decision is deviating significantly from the accepted beliefs. In the absence of clearly articulated values, there is a higher risk that forces or issues that can be harmful to the enterprise will influence leaders.

Above all, Warrior Leaders do what is right for the organization rather than what may be popular, expedient or convenient. The impact of some decisions is good—when the company is growing and adding jobs, for example, but other decisions, like when the company decides to contract and the result is to eliminate jobs, can adversely impact people. All job eliminations are tough, and the best that can be done is to ensure that the people adversely affected are treated with dignity and respect.

Remember when it comes to making tough decisions: Sometimes people do dumb things that are not logical. I can't remember the number of times I have coached a leader regarding a tough people decision where at some point I had to say, "You are lapsing into logic. Don't do that. What this person did is not logical." My other standard was, "Stop trying to rationalize the irrational." Why does a highly respected person with an impeccable career and record of achievement decide one day to misappropriate company funds, sexually harass a subordinate, or cover up egregious breaches of trust by a subordinate? You can try to rationalize why, but it does not change what the person did. It also does not change the decision that needs to be made.

Warrior Leaders Engender Diversity of Thought

Introspective leaders recognize that no matter how bright they are or how in touch they are with the business, there are always things to learn. Also, there are always several ways to assess opportunities and challenges. As such, they surround themselves with people from different backgrounds, and they encourage debate.

Leaders who surround themselves with people who are a mirror image of themselves in the way they think and analyze critical issues run the risk of making seriously flawed decisions. Such similar thinking may minimize alternatives. It also limits creativity and hurts the overall decision-making process. Usually leaders who surround themselves with like-thinking people value cohesiveness at the expense of healthy debate. Worse yet, insecure leaders will surround themselves with like-minded thinkers to avoid conflict and to ensure support for their position without regard to its merit.

Staying relevant with customers has become paramount in our global economy and even within the US borders, where our population is increasingly more diverse. The list below includes some marketing goofs that suggest a lack of diversity of thought or perspective in the decision-making process:

- Carmaker Chevrolet tried selling its model, the Nova, in Mexico. "No va" in Spanish translates as, "it does not go."[9]

- The "Got Milk?" marketing campaign did not play well with Hispanic customers either, since, for many, it translated as, "Are you lactating?"[10]

- Pepsi's marketing slogan "Come Alive with the Pepsi Generation" did not translate as intended into some Chinese dialects, where it meant, "Pepsi brings your ancestors back from the dead."[11]

- Finally, Clairol tried to market a curling iron with the name "Mist Stick." It turns out *mist* in German is slang for manure.[11]

Warrior Leaders believe that diverse perspectives and healthy debate results in better decisions. To achieve diverse perspectives requires that the team include people with different backgrounds. The differences can be gender, age, ethnicity or people from disparate parts of the country or even different work experiences. Additionally, healthy debate has to be nurtured. Building a diverse team does not automatically guarantee healthy debate. Warrior Leaders make it safe for people to speak their minds and provide their perspective. They do so by asking lots of questions of team members and by not denigrating or allowing others to denigrate perspectives that are different from conventional wisdom or the mainstream thought process.

Warrior Leaders Are Effective at Evaluating and Managing the Performance of Their Subordinates

In my years in Human Resources, I don't believe there is anything I found to be more unpopular among leaders than conducting performance reviews on their direct reports. It is an interesting dynamic because leaders are constantly evaluating the performance of the business, which is, by extension, the performance of the people in the business. But results are relatively easy to evaluate; it is behavior evaluation that causes all the consternation. Telling someone she missed her sales quota is relatively straightforward and of no surprise since the person being evaluated already knows that. Telling that person she missed her quota because she was not behaving in a manner that leads to results is another matter altogether. No one likes to tell someone else, "You are doing it wrong."

Leaders may not like evaluating performance, but Warrior Leaders recognize it as arguably one of the most important things they do. Below are the key things Warrior Leaders do that make them effective at evaluating a subordinate's performance.

Warrior Leaders:

- **Recognize that people's performance is the enterprise's performance.** The two are not mutually exclusive. Instead, they assess the person's individual performance in the context of the broader enterprise.

- **Don't keep inventory.** If something goes wrong they identify it, objectively analyze what happened and take steps to correct it. Whether the issue is behavioral or results-based, they discuss it with the individual as soon as possible and do not let it go without mention until the formal performance review. A widely accepted but often ignored rule is that there should be no surprises at the formal performance-review meeting. Organizations' performance-review processes vary greatly. Some require formal meetings periodically throughout the year and others only annually. Regardless of the timing, important issues should not be held in inventory to be revealed only at the formal review meeting.

- **Set clear goals and objectives.** In the absence of clear goals and objectives, subordinates will create their own or function without purpose. Warrior Leaders value measurement for themselves and their subordinates. Measurement begins with knowing what the goals are and the objectives necessary to achieve them. Warrior Leaders at the senior level set company and department goals and objectives. Warrior Leaders at the department or function level set goals for the work group and for individuals. The essence of any organization is clarity about where it is going and the ability to measure progress.

- **Are solution-oriented.** Placing blame on someone for something not done or something gone wrong is worthless and fixes nothing. It does, however, generate hard feelings and frustration. When things go wrong, as they often will, Warrior Leaders focus on understanding why it happened and how it can be resolved or prevented from happening again. That requires a focus on solutions that may, at times, include correcting the behavior of some individuals. If a discussion about behavior is appropriate, then it should occur, but the focus should be on solutions and not who is to blame.

  Imagine working in a department or company where any time anything of consequence goes wrong, leadership looks for someone to blame. In a blame-focused environment, the only thing that suffers is performance. People will not stretch, innovate or care; they will bide their time to get out as soon as possible.

- **Are direct and objective about results and rely on facts to support their conclusions.** While results are relatively easy to quantify, behaviors are often hard to quantify. Over the past 20 years, much effort has gone into developing competencies that are clusters of behaviors valued by the organization. For example, most companies that use competencies will define leadership behaviors like communications, teamwork, developing and leading strategies or people, etc. The leader then rates the subordinate based on how they observed the person's behavior in relation to the behaviors used to define that competency. Whether your company uses competencies or not, rating behavior requires judgment. What the leader judges to be poor, the subordinate may judge to be good. Certainly, attempts should be made by the leader to develop a common ground of what is good vs. what is poor. That said, some employees simply won't agree with the leader's assessment. In those situations, the Warrior Leader is satisfied with the subordinate's understanding of a rating. Agreeing to disagree over a rating is okay as long as the employee understands what is expected in the future. It is just as important to be as direct and clear as possible when describing what the person is or isn't doing. This does not mean you should attack the person or label them. "Direct" is not the same as "pejorative."

"Prior to becoming an entrepreneur, the worst boss I ever had was arrogant, aloof and a terrible listener. He didn't care about people. I remember that receiving a performance review was a total joke. First, he never spent time with me so had no idea how I did my job. He was not engaged but expected me to accept the performance review as accurate. To make it worse, he would tell me things I was not doing well but offered no facts to support the conclusion and no guidance or development advice."
— CARMEN DeCARRIER, McDONALD'S FRANCHISEE

- **Recognize and act on the presumption that poor performers are a reflection on themselves, especially if the leader put the poor performer in place.** A leader being too deferential sometimes leads to dire consequences. The same concept applies here: The Warrior Leader does not allow poor performers to linger. That does not mean firing someone at the first sign of poor performance. It may mean providing more training or moving the person to another role more in line with their strengths. But if it is purely poor performance without mitigating circumstances, the Warrior Leader makes the tough call and terminates the individual.

Subordinates pay close attention to what actions leaders take regarding poor performers. People value fairness but are not patient with leaders who allow chronic poor performers to bring down the effectiveness of a department or to adversely impact the department's reputation. Accordingly, subordinates hold leaders responsible for tolerating poor performers.

- **Trust subordinates unless they create a reason not to.** Knowing that the boss trusts you is an incredible catalyst for most people. Working for a boss who does not trust your judgment or work product creates uncertainty for the individual and, for many, is unnerving. An absence of trust causes some people to question everything they do. The Warrior Leader provides good direction, ensures the subordinate has the skill and resources necessary to perform, and gets out of the way while periodically checking in with the subordinate to ensure all is well.

Leaders who, as a rule of thumb, don't trust subordinates tend to micro-manage. Poor performers, unfortunately, require a higher level of oversight until performance improves or they move on. But to micro-manage as a standard method of operating results in a host of adverse consequences, including:

  - Discouraging creativity
  - Discouraging initiative
  - Creating work paralysis
  - Impeding individual development

- **Recognize the importance of pointing out why subordinates did something well.** One of the most often-missed development opportunities occurs when a leader recognizes good performance but does not point out why. When good performance occurs, many leaders simply recognize it and miss the opportunity to reinforce the specific behaviors that led to the high-quality performance. When people are recognized for superior performance, they feel good, but the leader should not assume that the subordinate understands why. Specifically, the leader should be clear with the subordinate about what they did that, in the leader's judgment, caused the fine results. Doing so will encourage the individual to repeat the effective behaviors.

- **Have empathy for subordinates but are not paralyzed by it.** We all go through tough times at some point. The Warrior Leader feels empathy for a subordinate going through rough times and will do what they can to help, but at some point, for some people, a tough decision may be the only option left. The workplace does not stop to wait for people facing adversity. Customers, shareholders and co-workers still have expectations. People are tolerant of a person's plight only to a point. Every situation has its limits of tolerance, and, the more critical the role, the more pressure there is for the person to return to being fully functional as soon as possible. Unfortunately, that does not always happen. In such cases, leaders are faced with having to make decisions that the person experiencing the adversity may not always understand or appreciate. Again, it may not mean terminating the person but might mean placing them on medical or personal leave or transferring them to another job that may involve a demotion. Another option, in many companies, is to offer the employee help through an "Employee Assistance Program." These programs are confidential and offer a variety of services to employees with serious medical, personal or financial problems.

- **Recognize and act on the premise that performance is a period-by-period dynamic.** Subordinates that performed well and were highly rated one year may not perform as well the following year and, accordingly, should not be highly rated. The reverse is also true: poor performance one year does not mean the individual can't turn it around and perform well the following year.

On this topic, I'd like to narrow down the focus to people who do the same job for years, even decades. This is not as common in this day and age as it used to be, but these folks do exist. Anyone who does the same job for years and years should be really good or even great at what they do, otherwise it begs the question, "Why are they still doing it?" This is not to suggest that people aren't capable of consistently performing at a high level. There are many people who do. But to perform at the highest levels year in and year out is truly unique. Think about this in terms of your favorite author. He or she may have written several great books, but most likely, at some point, a mediocre, or even a bad book appeared. The point is that Warrior Leaders call it as it is, even with the people who have been in the same role year after year. Additionally, Warrior Leaders expect more from people who have been proficient in the same role for a long time. If a person has mastered a role over the years, they should be in a position to recommend more efficient ways to get things done, to be a mentor or train others. Warrior Leaders expect a lot from all their employees, but especially from those who have mastered their role and are in a position to make more of an impact on the enterprise.

For most leaders, the job of assessing performance and conducting performance evaluations with subordinates is akin to root canal. However, without it, the enterprise is rudderless. People need to understand what is expected of them and how their actions support or detract from the goals of the organization.

Warrior Leaders Are Adept at Managing Teams

Teams in an organization can be incredibly valuable and can also be an abysmal waste of time and money. Teams come in many forms, both small and large. There are intradepartmental as well as cross-functional teams. There are ongoing teams along with *ad hoc* teams. Warrior Leaders know the added value that can be gained from teams but are judicious about creating them or volunteering subordinates to participate in cross-functional efforts. Specifically they:

- **Recognize that a team cannot solve all tough problems.** Some problems need to be solved by the individual decision-makers at the root of the issue or at the leadership level. Certainly, getting input from key people is important, but some things should not be delegated to a team.

- **Do not create a team or volunteer staff to a team unless there is a clear charter that defines the purpose of the team, including specific deliverables and time frames.** Deliverables should clearly state how the efforts of the team are going to benefit the department or enterprise. Hopefully, you will never be assigned to a team that takes an inordinate amount of time to figure out what their purpose and goals are. I have been in that situation, and I don't wish it on anybody. There are even Dumb Ass leaders who purposely form a team to avoid or delay making decisions.

"The best teams start with leaders who create a positive energy and alignment, and who drive results. Descriptors of successful teams are focused, passionate, committed, fun, balanced, high energy, creative and innovative. There is also a clearly defined start and finish timeline.

"The members of the best performing teams recognize they are each significant in driving the team's results and fully engaged in the process and the outcome. They 'own' it and learn from each other. They seek individual learning and express their opinions freely. There is mutual respect among team members.

"The ineffective teams fail to achieve results for a variety of reasons: the failure of leadership, weak or uncommitted team members, or a vision that is beyond the ability of the team to execute. Teams need a clear SMART (Specific, Measurable, Attainable, Relevant and Time Bound) platform. Going blindly into the night relying mainly on 'hope' usually ends badly."
— Brian Unger, Former Chief Operating Officer, Einstein Noah Restaurant Group, Inc.

- **Gage the level of commitment in the organization by how the team is supported.** Predictably, uncommitted team members delay progress by not attending meetings. Some do not follow up on commitments or may function on their own time frame vis-a-vis the timelines of the team. Warrior Leaders ensure that if a team is worth forming, it has participants who are fully committed. Full commitment requires that other leaders in the organization, especially those volunteering staff, recognize the importance of the team and are supportive of it.

- **Eliminate barriers as necessary for the team to succeed.**
  Barriers can come in many forms. For example, if a team
  includes an uncommitted member, the Warrior Leader steps
  in and ensures the person becomes committed or leaves.
  People outside the team can also be a barrier. Many teams
  conduct research or fact-finding that requires cooperation
  from staff throughout the organization. In some cases, the
  request by the team to someone outside the team may go
  to the bottom of the priority list. In these situations, the
  Warrior Leader steps in to ensure that staff throughout the
  organization is engaged and appropriately prioritize the
  requests of legitimate teams.

Some organizations produce their own problems by forming
teams for the flimsiest of reasons. Becoming team-happy, they
believe anything of any consequence needs to be resolved
by a team. There could be so many teams operating in the
organization or department that it is impossible for anyone
to appropriately prioritize requests. I was in an organization
that literally went from one extreme over the use of teams to
the other extreme almost overnight after a change of Chief
Executive Officer. Before the change of CEO, each department
in the company made major decisions affecting the business
without including other departments. After the change, every
major decision had to be made through cross-functional teams.
It was an utter disaster and resulted in yet another change
at the CEO level before the company found the appropriate
balance regarding the use of teams.

Warrior Leaders are judicious about building teams, and, when
they do, they give the team the support needed to succeed,
including the elimination of barriers.

- **Select the right people to be on teams, including using teams as a form of development.** Who leaders assign to teams speaks volumes about their judgment. Warrior Leaders recognize that teams are a great development opportunity for some people. A cross-functional team provides an excellent opportunity to meet people from other departments and to learn about other functions. Team members may also get the opportunity to meet senior leaders or present their findings to those they would otherwise not have interactions with. In most large organizations, even intradepartmental teams can be valuable. If you work in a company that has locations throughout the U.S. or the world, chances are most functional disciplines will place staff at both the corporate headquarters and in the field offices. Therefore, it is likely there are many people in your functional discipline that you may never have the opportunity to work with unless you happen to be assigned to a team.

  Warrior Leaders may also utilize a team to put someone in a leadership role. The opportunity to observe someone in a temporary leadership capacity is an effective way to assess the individual's potential for more permanent or broader leadership roles.

- **Assess the effectiveness of teams they have created and make the necessary changes to ensure the team's effectiveness.** Many teams have a hard time getting started. Teams go through several phases before they can be productive. Some teams never reach an appropriate level of effectiveness. As such, the Warrior Leader regularly monitors the progress of a team and makes the changes necessary to keep it viable—either that, or they disband it. Changes may be a matter of revising the charter of the team, improving resources, changing team members, bringing in new members with a specific background or expertise, and, if necessary, changing the leader.

Think about a time you were on a team. Did you ever look around the room and try to estimate the dollars the team members spent debating or planning? The costs of the salaries of team members alone can be significant. Add to that other resources that the team may be using, and the costs continue to mount. Sometimes teams are ill-conceived, not productive or formed at the wrong time. In those instances, it is best to cut the losses and disband the group.

- **Engender an atmosphere where team members don't care who gets the credit.** It is amazing what can be accomplished when there are multiple people working on solving difficult issues or creating something special and no one cares who gets the credit. When people's primary focus is on the issue at hand, rather than looking good or being recognized, great things can happen.

I don't know how many people over the years have been involved in trying to find cures for serious illnesses. In many cases, when there is a medical breakthrough and cures are found, credit is assigned to someone, but think of all the people who were involved who no one ever knows about. Did all the people involved not seek credit? Of course not, but I truly believe that most did not seek it. Most significant breakthroughs in science and business would never have come to fruition without the many people who simply focused on what they had to do rather than on glory.

"I've worked on many teams around the country. What makes the good ones special is when team members work together, respect each other and are not afraid to have open, honest conversations. It is also recognizing that everyone is on the same team and wants to do something for the greater good of the company. It is realizing that if one of us wins, then all of us win."

— Vicki Guster-Hines, Regional Vice President of Operations, McDonald's Corporation

In the Introduction, I mentioned that all but one of the friends or colleagues who provided perspectives and stories for this book were seasoned leaders. The one exception is a young man I have known since he was a freshman in high school with my son. He is, in my opinion, a bright, thoughtful and hardworking person who learned a tough but valuable lesson early in his career. Here is what Jay Gillette, Securities Auditor, had to share:

"I was hired directly out of college to work for a moderately sized financial services firm. Both my department head and I had played college football, so we had an immediate connection. I could tell that he wanted me to get better so I could have a better life. It was the general consensus that he would look out for all of his employees and ensure they kept their jobs as long as they achieved the results. His leadership and professionalism greatly shaped the culture of the department. Everyone completed their tasks in a timely and thorough manner; there was a spirit of teamwork and cooperation, and the work environment was fun and professional.

"Unfortunately, the firm's upper management did not deem our department's employees to be important. Other

departments received significant bonuses while we received none. What's more, members of our team did not receive regular pay raises. As a result, three out of the top four people in our department left the company for better-paying opportunities. One of the people who left the company was our revered boss.

"Upper management hired a new department head who set up interviews with everyone as his first order of business. We did not know at the time that we were all interviewing for our jobs. Within a matter of weeks, one employee was fired, and everyone began to feel like they had to work differently to show how important they were. It created unhealthy competition and a backstabbing type of environment. Everyone, of course, wanted to keep their jobs: for some, even if it was at the expense of others. The once-friendly and team-oriented environment became a thing of the past.

"The new department head was not personable and was socially awkward. He could not relate to his employees and created a top-down culture that was not at all inclusive. He did not respect his direct reports, and he consistently devalued the work of everyone in the department. I believe that his biggest weakness was that he was unable or unwilling to relate to his employees on a personal level, and therefore he looked at them as pawns and not as people.

"In a matter of a few months, I began interviewing and accepted a job at another company. Several of my co-workers also left to pursue better opportunities."

Warrior Leaders Are Adept at Selecting and Developing Other Warriors

Most companies, especially those that are publicly traded, are all about profitable growth. To grow profitably requires talented people and the ability to replenish and develop them as the enterprise expands. Therefore the ability to consistently identify talent becomes an essential attribute for leaders. Warrior Leaders are adept at identifying great people and helping them to develop their professional skills. Further, they love to find and develop people who are better than they are. People who are brighter and more creative do not threaten them. Rather, they view them as catalysts to accomplish the goals of the enterprise.

Warrior Leaders recognize that consistent results and growth cannot be achieved with mediocre talent. Sustained success requires a pipeline of committed, hard-working and bright people. A word about what I mean by bright in the context of an organization: People can be book smart and lack an ounce of common, people or business sense. Just because a given discipline may require X amount of education or some professional certification does not make a person bright in the context of an organization. These people certainly possess a level of intelligence sufficient to obtain a degree or certification, but when it comes to thriving in a dynamic environment, they may not have the common sense or intuition. In short, they may be a Subject Matter Expert but are very limited in terms of being an asset in the broader sense of the enterprise. Warrior Leaders seek individuals to develop who are bright in the broader context.

There are many ways to develop people. None is more valuable, in my opinion, than giving people opportunities to experience new things. In addition to teams, special projects, research, job swapping, working side by side with a subordinate and special assignments are all examples of development opportunities that engender learning and professional growth. Within global companies, the list may also include international assignments. None of these are to suggest that book learning or, as another example, professional seminars, are of no value. These, too, have their place, but I strongly believe there is no substitute for experience. In order to provide employees with these development opportunities, the Warrior Leader must possess the courage to support people and, when he needs to, accept failure.

Another way Warrior Leaders help to develop people is to let them go. That may mean losing a great person to a transfer or promotion to another department or area of the company. As hard as it is to lose a great employee, hoarding talent does not encourage development and is not good for the company overall. That being said, letting them go has to make sense for the employee, the department they are leaving and the department they are going to. An opportunity for promotion may be great for the employee and the department that is getting them, but the timing may be detrimental to the department or the work they would be leaving behind.

Warrior Leaders believe that short of it creating a catastrophe (which is seldom the case), they err on the side of what is good for the employee. Organizations that put people first in such circumstances usually develop a level of commitment from people that is difficult to duplicate. A key tenet of letting people go, even if the timing is not right, is to always set up a succession plan, specifically: Who are the people available to step up when you lose a key person? Warrior Leaders are constantly identifying talent to ensure they have successors to follow in the footsteps of key players. Accordingly, Warrior Leaders will seldom, if ever, stand in the way of career-growth opportunities for high-caliber people.

Finally Warrior Leaders use inclusiveness as a means of developing and optimizing productivity. They discuss important issues and ask for input from subordinates. They keep subordinates involved about important information that may impact the department or the company and ask for their input. Likewise, they may also discuss challenging issues with subordinates. In the process, they gain valuable insights they otherwise would not know about the subordinates. When employees are more aware, they can help the leader more, for example when the leader is absent and issues arise. Information is a great source of empowerment. There are some things that are confidential that a leader cannot discuss with subordinates, but most things are not. Some leaders hoard information and share very little with subordinates. That usually leads to unproductive work environments and can be a source of confusion and frustration. A leader that does not share is not optimizing or developing talent. Think of situations when your leader has been inaccessible and you are asked by customers or other departments for information they assume you should have. It happens all too often.

> *"The best direct boss I ever had was my first sales manager. He always talked about what makes a great salesperson, using examples of what he had done in his career to achieve sales, and he was very good at it. Not only did he coach me, he would go on sales calls with me and actually do what he told me. I have never forgotten what I learned and have used his teachings in everything I do, not only in business sales, but in all kinds of negotiations, both business and personal, as well. I learned that a good boss not only teaches, but also demonstrates."*
>
> — THOMAS E. KERESTES, FORMER GLOBAL COMMODITIES MANAGER, BRITISH PETROLEUM CORPORATION

Warrior Leaders Respect the Personal Lives of Subordinates

Leaders need to be demanding of results; it is another thing to be demanding of superfluous things in a way that infringes on personal lives. Warrior Leaders recognize and value the fact that work is only one aspect of a person's life. Obviously, work is a very important aspect, but it should not be all-absorbing. There are times when the demands on the enterprise are such that long hours are required and expected to achieve what is necessary. Sometimes these demands can go on for extended periods of time. This is the nature of working in a fast-paced, competitive and results-oriented environment. But there are limits to what leaders can expect, and the line of demarcation begins with not encroaching on personal time and lives.

There are leaders who create events or situations where subordinates are supposed to be present for no good reason. These superfluous expectations take time away from family, significant others, friends or even a life-balancing hobby. Warrior Leaders recognize this and the importance of life away from work as a means for people to achieve balance in their lives.

"I was in a managerial role and very busy. There were a lot of things going on and a lot of moving pieces. My wife and I had decided to take a vacation to Disneyworld when our twin girls were about four, and everyone was excited. My boss at the time was one of those bosses who cared more for me as an individual than as an employee. We arrived in Florida on Monday afternoon. I had continued checking my voice mails to ensure I knew about any important things that may be going on, and on Tuesday morning my boss called and said, 'You're on vacation with your family—you need to be on vacation with your family—they need all of you.' I told him that I was focusing on my family and the vacation. He quickly replied by asking, 'Then why isn't your voice mail filled up already? I know you're checking it—STOP IT, STOP IT NOW and don't let me catch you making any phone calls, sending emails, or listening to voice mail. You need this time with your girls and wife!' Then he hung up. This incident left an indelible impression on me."

— BUD LORD, DIRECTOR OF OPERATIONS, McDONALD'S CORPORATION

Warrior Leaders Do Not Allow the Emergencies of Others to Become Their Own

At times people make mistakes of commission. By that I mean that, in their zeal to do their best, sometimes people do things that lead to unintended consequences that create problems for others. Nobody appreciates problems, especially those caused by others. Most of us are somewhat tolerant when the problems are based on commission and good intent. However, when people create problems for others through negligence or omission, the tolerance level is very low. People, in general, show a low tolerance level for someone else's emergency becoming their own. Unfortunately, if the nature of the problem is potentially harmful to the department or enterprise, it has to be addressed. Warrior Leaders will do what is right to address these issues but also make it clear to whoever created problems of omission or negligence that it is unacceptable and will not be tolerated in the future. They will also provide support to subordinates who are adversely impacted.

Warrior Leaders Demand Focus on the Highest Value Activities

Some leaders don't know how to say no and therefore over-commit themselves and their people. Some leaders are addicted to activity. Their logic is that if there is a lot of work and a lot of things going on, they are doing well. The reality is that unfocused activity is just that. Warrior Leaders constantly ensure that they are focused on the few but most value-added activities that will have the biggest influence on achieving results.

Corporations are complex, with different functions trying to do their part to contribute to the success of the enterprise. To achieve true focus, all functions within an enterprise have to be on the same page regarding key strategies and the actions necessary to achieve them. This is harder to do than it may appear. First, it requires clear communication about the strategies. More importantly, it requires commitment from everyone on the few key strategies. One way to obtain commitment is to require each major department within the enterprise to clearly articulate how what they do or what they may be asking other departments to do will contribute to the achievement of the key strategies. If departments are recommending or imposing expectations on others that do not contribute to the achievement of strategies, Warrior Leaders challenge them and, if appropriate, eliminate these activities.

At times, in order to retain focus, a shift in resources may be required. Fiduciary responsibilities may not contribute anything to producing better products or services, but to ignore those invites legal and safety concerns. Accordingly, the enterprise must have the necessary resources to ensure that fiduciary responsibilities are executed but never lose sight of the primary strategies. For anything that does not fall under the fiduciary responsibility umbrella, every function needs to ask, "Is what we do contributing to the key strategies of the enterprise?" Warrior Leaders ensure that activities that are not essential to execution of the key strategies are eliminated or pushed down the priority list.

Think of your daily life. Most of us have literally hundreds of things that we wish we could do and that we have to do. Those of us who do not focus and prioritize invariably fall into one of two camps. You try to be all things to all people and soon realize that you are not doing anything well and pleasing no one. Then there are those who do only what they like to do and ignore the rest. That usually leads to some disaster down the road. Whether it is your personal or corporate life, to succeed requires clear strategies and goals. The fewer goals and strategies you pursue, the better. Ask yourself: Would I rather do a lot of things at a mediocre level or would I rather do fewer things at an excellent or outstanding level?

To agree and commit to the highest value-added strategies and activities for the enterprise is important. However, regular and brutally honest calibration about progress or failures is also important.

If changes in resources or tactics are necessary, they should be made. Blind commitment to strategies that are not working is a drain on the organization's people and its assets.

> *"My boss, who I considered a great leader, had a great knack for emphasizing the organization's issues of highest priority and applying the greatest portion of the organization's energy to achieving those ends. He took well the advice of one old sage who is quoted as saying, 'Don't waste your time and energy stamping on the ants while the elephants are running all over you.'"*
>
> — Charles G. Zeisser, Former VP of Human Resources, SSM Healthcare of Wisconsin

Warrior Leaders Are Positive and Exude Positive Energy

A large part of any leader's role is to solve problems, remove barriers and deal with unpleasant issues. There are stretches of time when the leader's role can be burdened by negative situations or issues. At these times, the Warrior Leaders shine the brightest. Regardless of how unpleasant or challenging the circumstances may be, the Warrior Leader exudes positive energy rather than being consumed by the negatives. This does not mean that the leader is oblivious to the negatives or tries to spin communications to make negative things appear good. It means that they recognize the problem, deal with it, look for the lessons learned and move on in a positive manner.

Finally, Warrior Leaders look for the positive attributes in their colleagues and subordinates. They build relationships on what is positive about people rather than focus on the negatives or the weaknesses that people may have. Certainly with subordinates they will try to change the negatives but always with a focus on leading with people's strengths as a foundation to improving the weaknesses.

Warrior Leaders Are Adept at Conveying Compelling Vision

Vision is difficult for many people to grasp, especially those who do not possess active imaginations or the ability to process ideas that are new or intangible. Some are also limited by their reluctance to change. The bigger the perceived change, the more resistant to it they become. As such, it is imperative for leaders to be able to convey a compelling vision of where and how they see the future of the enterprise going.

Warrior Leaders are grounded in reality but not governed or paralyzed by it. They retain the ability to look at a future that can be very different from the reality of today: A future that is exciting and remarkable for the enterprise, its employees and shareholders. More importantly, they have the ability to describe their vision in a way that gets even some of the naysayers on board and excited about it. They do so by, first and foremost, exhibiting their personal commitment and enthusiasm about the vision. As importantly, they are realistic about the challenges to be overcome in order to achieve the vision and what resources will be required to do so. Finally, Warrior Leaders lay out the high-level steps that will need to be taken to move the enterprise from today's reality to the future vision. Who would have thought in 1961 that President John F. Kennedy's vision to put a man in the moon within a decade would ever be realized? Astronaut Neil Armstrong of the Apollo 11 mission set foot on the lunar surface in July of 1969.[12]

Of course, regardless of how eloquently it is presented, not everyone in an enterprise will be sold on a given vision. There are always detractors, but the Warrior Leaders ensure that enough people in the organization, especially other key leaders, see the vision as compelling and commit to seeing it to fruition.

"Think about how many speeches or discussions that you've been present for at your company (and may have even listened to a few of them). From the very beginning of the remarks, you can tell if that leader/manager is simply mouthing the words of their Communications Assistant. You typically hear a series of updates about results, a look at what's immediately ahead of us and a reminder of what we need to execute, and a story or two that is shared which relates to best practices regarding where we want to go. That formula is pretty tried and true and becomes the expectation and norm. Contrast that with listening to a leader who has and shares a cogent narrative about his/her vision for the future. Every time that leader speaks, you're struck by the consistency and passion of the message. You're struck by how they have thoughtfully sequenced the plans and events to lead us down that path to achieve that vision. Those leaders always seem to take you out of your comfort zone. They share learning from other companies within your industry and, more importantly, out of your industry. They minimize the 'corporate speak' and inspire you to think differently.

"Another hallmark about these visionary leaders is their curiosity. I have found that the worst managers are those who are not open to be taught by the people beneath them. Call it lack of humility, ego, lack of self-confidence; it is amazing how some managers in very high positions think they possess all the answers. The higher you rise in an organization, the less truth you will hear. If you isolate yourself or rely on a small cadre of people who always agree with you, you will ultimately become the barrier. You will create untold frustration for those who are trying to execute a *plan that was concocted without the input from those who ultimately have to execute it.*

"The inspirational leader is able to shepherd a lot of ideas and perspectives, deal well with ambiguity and define a common future."
— MIKE ANDRES, CHAIRMAN AND CHIEF EXECUTIVE OFFICER, LOGAN'S ROADHOUSE INC.

Warrior Leaders Reveal Great Character

Leadership begins with character. *Webster's* dictionary defines character as "one of the attributes or features that make up and distinguish an individual."[13] According to that definition, character can be either good or bad. For the purpose of this book, I refer to good character, which includes attributes like moral courage, honesty, being humble, caring and appreciative and having integrity and empathy. In the context of the corporate world, it also includes the ability to make the tough decisions. It includes putting the enterprise, and its people and shareholders, above one's own personal priorities. Finally, it includes ensuring that employees and customers are treated fairly and with the utmost respect. In a leadership role anyone lacking any of these attributes is out of place.

"Leaders never compromise their personal integrity. Consistent with the theme those leaders are difference-makers in an organization, leaders can motivate and inspire because they are respected. This respect is earned, not only by their unique perspective on business, their visionary thinking and inspiring communication, but also by their personal integrity. What a privilege it is to have people follow you, and what a shame it is to disappoint your followers. This can be done by creating an environment that is prone to gossip

and innuendo, by not maintaining the confidence of those who entrust you with deeply personal information and by comfortably telling untruths and half-truths in the face of difficult situations or questions. The sole motivation to this gap in integrity is self-preservation or to maintain or build upon some real or imaginary power base.

"Leaders are most interested in seeing others get the credit and seeing others succeed. They understand this because some strong leader in their past had that attitude and approach, saw the potential in them and worked to put them in a position to realize their potential. They want to offer that same opportunity to the people they lead."

— Mike Andres, Chairman and Chief Executive Officer, Logan's Roadhouse Inc.

As with the discussion on Warriors, this list of Warrior Leader traits is also arguably long. But again I submit that there is nothing on the list that is special; there is nothing magical or ethereal. As with the attributes and behaviors of Warriors, to be a Warrior Leader requires honest introspection about opportunities, help from trusted colleagues and a commitment to work on the things that need refinement.

For Warrior Leaders, regular doses of brutal honesty and calibration are important. Some people do all the right things to get to senior leadership levels and then forget where they came from or what got them there. Worse yet, some begin to suffer from a bad case of omnipotence and quickly lose touch with reality. Warrior Leaders seek perspective on how they are doing. Specifically, they want to know how customers and employees perceive them. Warrior leaders believe that leadership is a privilege and act on the adage that "to whom much is given, much is expected."

CHAPTER SUMMARY

Warrior Leaders:

- *Keep their egos in check*
- *Value other leaders but are not overly deferential to them*
- *Understand that most people need to be led but do not abuse the privilege*
- *Are charismatic, but not flamboyant, communicators*
- *Keep people informed about the things that matter*
- *Are great listeners*
- *Are decisive and courageous about addressing the tough issues*
- *Engender diversity of thoughts*
- *Are effective at evaluating and managing the performance of their subordinates*
- *Are adept at managing teams*
- *Are adept at selecting and developing other Warriors*
- *Respect the personal lives of subordinates*
- *Do not allow the emergencies of others to become their own*
- *Demand focus on the highest-value activities*
- *Are positive and exude positive energy*
- *Are adept at conveying compelling vision*
- *Reveal great character*

CHAPTER THREE

The Dumb Asses

How does someone become a Dumb Ass? Are they born that way, or do they simply deteriorate into one? For the purposes of this book, Dumb Asses are not people who are intellectually challenged so much as people who ought to know better but consistently do dumb things. It turns out that people deteriorate into Dumb Asses.

To calibrate this breed of Barbarian, let's review some behaviors of Dumb Asses in everyday lives. Here are a few examples:

Airplane travel dumb stuff:

- The person at the ticket counter who takes an inordinate amount of time making or changing arrangements that should have been done online or on the phone. The person is oblivious to the fact that there is a long line of travelers with a limited amount of time to make their flight. If that isn't bad enough, when the insensitive, time-consuming traveler is finally done, he starts chitchatting with the ticket agent, further delaying everyone else in line. I'm not sure who the bigger Dumb Ass is in this scenario, the time-consuming traveler or the ticket agent.

- The person who believes the bathrooms are theirs and theirs alone. Most airplanes are not equipped with an abundance of lavatories, and, especially on long flights, they are at a premium. There is usually at least one selfish person on every flight who believes she can take as much time in the toilet as she likes without regard to the other people on board.

- The person with the oversized backpack who is also pushing a suitcase on rollers through the narrow airplane aisle. To make matters worse, these people are constantly pivoting from side to side and every time they turn, anyone sitting in an aisle seat is either clocked in the head by the backpack or gets the roller bag slammed into their knees. Most of these people also manage to walk past their assigned seat so they have to reverse course and inflict pain on the aisle dwellers all over again.

- The person sitting next to you who likes to chitchat about nothing in particular for the full length of the flight. You have your head-set on and a book open, sending a very clear signal that you do not want to be disturbed, but nothing deters them. I have even tried pulling out a rosary and pretended to be praying, unfortunately to no avail.

Miscellaneous dumb stuff:

- The person on the cell phone who picks the most quiet of places, like a doctor's office or the library, to yak away so that everyone within earshot is forced to hear their annoying conversations.

- The person who gets off the escalator and comes to a dead stop while everyone behind them is trying to get off.

- The person who blocks the elevator door trying to get in before people have the chance to exit.

- We can't forget the people who talk through an entire movie. These are the same people that are constantly kicking the back of your seat.

You might say that most of the things above are innocent, and I would agree. They might be annoying, but they cause no real harm. Truth is that 99.9 percent of the population has probably been guilty of at least one of these dumb acts at some point. Does that make them Dumb Asses? No. The Dumb Asses are the people that do a bunch of these things on a regular basis. Doing thoughtless things over and over invariably leads to doing things that are more serious and can cause harm. Take, for example, the imprudent things that people do while driving their cars.

- The person who drives way below the speed limit in the left passing lane. They are being passed by everyone on the right lane but won't move over.

- The person driving six inches from your rear bumper when you are already doing seventy in a fifty-five-mile-an-hour zone, but you are blocked by a truck and can't move to the right lane.

- The people who are unaware or don't care that turn signals were invented a long time ago. Or the ones who see you turn your signal on and speed up so you cannot switch lanes.

- The people distracted by things they should not be doing while driving. According to a study by the National Highway Traffic Safety Administration, the most common types of distractions include but are not limited to the following:

  - Texting
  - Talking on a cell phone
  - Looking at an object or event outside of the vehicle
  - Reading
  - Eating[1]

For me, anyone who drives and regularly gets distracted by the things I listed above goes beyond being a mortal Dumb Ass; instead, they are in the company of the Stunningly Stupid.

When you look at the lists, do they suggest that only people of limited intellectual capacity participate in such activities? Of course not—people you know do these things, as do teachers, engineers and doctors. It is neither a gender, nor a cultural, issue. Those who do these things regularly are not intellectually challenged. Rather, they are simply down-to-the-bone Dumb Asses. They know they should not do these things, but they do them anyway.

Below are some of the behaviors that we see in the corporate arena from co-workers who habitually do dumb things.

Dumb Asses Rationalize Failure and Are Blame-Oriented

Dumb Asses are prone to rationalize why something went wrong or something did not work. These behaviors can vary, depending on the enterprise. Below are some generic examples.

- The person who did a lousy job on the report but blames not being given the specifics.

- The person who misses the deadline on critical work and then compounds it by not telling anyone it will be missed. They then blame everyone else for the delay.

- The person who does not respond to important emails or voicemails in a timely manner. Some of these people are so habitual about not responding that, whenever I identified one of these chronic procrastinators, I went out of my way to confirm receipt of messages whenever possible. What I learned is that some of these people did not read emails or listen to voice mail at all. However, when confronted, they had a litany of reasons why they were unable to get to their messages. Furthermore, some of these habitual deflectors would lose track of how many times they had used the same excuse. (Sometimes I would count how many times a person's grandmother died.)

- The person, often a leader, who ignores bad work or even unsafe work conditions in the hope that the problems will disappear. As they say, "hope is not a strategy," and invariably, problems ignored come back to haunt.

Creating lame excuses for failure is not good; compounding failure by playing the blame game is truly dumb. People who go even farther and claim it was not their responsibility when it clearly was are truly a rarified breed of dumb. When a person is known to be an expert player of the "Blame or Shirk-the-Responsibility" game, what they are actually doing is telling everyone that they can't be counted on for anything. They also can't be trusted, because you never know when the person playing the "Blame" game is going to point the finger at you.

When serious or even tragic things occur as a result of someone's ignorance or negligence, the truth can sometimes get very murky, especially when there are multiple entities involved and the dynamics include the "Blame or Shirk-the-Responsibility" games. Below are some examples of situations that are sad, but true. Not having been part of these situations, it is difficult to be 100 percent certain about what truly happened, but by reading the accounts of the incidents, it does not take much imagination to conclude that some degree of placing blame and/or shirking responsibilities was at play:

- One of the saddest incidents I can recall of things having truly gone bad was the Space Shuttle Challenger Disaster, with teacher Christa McAuliffe on board. As you probably know, that space shuttle exploded shortly after takeoff, killing the entire crew. NASA, and a presidential commission, known as the Rogers Commission, investigated the matter. It was determined that faulty O-rings designed to contain hot high-pressure gases were the primary cause of the accident. Where the incident becomes inexplicable is when it was revealed that the manufacturer, Morton Thiokol, of the O-rings knew well prior to launch that there were serious concerns about them. If that was the case, why was the Shuttle allowed to take off? Was it poor communication or other more questionable mistakes? Whatever the case, the sad conclusion is that the incident was preventable.[2, 3]

- After years of running a Ponzi scheme that resulted in the loss of billions of dollars for thousands of investors, Bernie Madoff pleaded guilty and was sent to jail. I guess that the evidence of guilt was so overwhelming that even an Egomaniac like Bernie couldn't deny the truth or pass the blame. That he thought he could get away with it puts him in the category of the "Stunningly Stupid." He was sentenced to more than

100 years in prison (but somehow that does not seem long enough). What is also troubling about this case is that the Securities and Exchange Commission had received warnings about Madoff as early as 1999 but his scheme did not unravel till 2008. Among Madoff's victims were individual investors and charities.[4, 5]

- In the spring of 2011, twenty-nine miners died in the Upper Big Branch Mine in West Virginia. The Mine Safety and Health Administration had cited the company operating the mine, Massey Energy, for multiple violations. Some of the violations were for failure to comply with and/or correct previous violations. After the investigation of the incident, Massey was cited for hundreds more violations and millions of dollars in fines.[6, 7]

- Several historic catastrophes have involved ships, among them the Titanic, the Exxon Valdez and, of more recent vintage, the cruise ship Costa Concordia. All are fraught with what appear to be some very dumb things taking place. Although it sank more than one hundred years ago, most people today know about the Titanic. The ship hit an iceberg and sank, killing more than 1,500 hundred of the roughly 2,200 people on board. What some may not know is that the ship was equipped with enough lifeboats to accommodate fewer than 1,200 people. Furthermore, as the disaster played out, many of the vessels cast off filled below their capacity leaving behind hundreds, including women and children, to drown or die of exposure in the freezing waters of the North Atlantic Ocean.[8]

The Exxon Valdez oil spill, although not involving loss of human life, was an enormous environmental disaster that caused considerable loss of wildlife. More than 10 million gallons of oil spilled into Prince William Sound. Joseph Hazelwood, the captain of the ship, was accused but not convicted of being under the influence of alcohol. He was convicted and fined for negligent discharge of oil. At least two other people were in the wheelhouse at the time immediately prior to the accident occurring. It is unclear who was responsible for the ship running aground on a reef but Captain Hazelwood was in his quarters when the spill occurred.[9]

As of this writing, the disaster involving the cruise ship Costa Concordia is still playing itself out. The ship's captain was Francesco Schettino. The ship ran aground on January of 2012 off the coast of Giglio, Italy. The stories from crew and some passengers differ greatly from Schettino's story. Time and the courts will sift through the truth. In the meantime, more than 30 people died. Schettino is alleged to have been safely on a lifeboat while hundreds of passengers and crew were still on the foundering ship.[10, 11]

• Another preventable and catastrophic event was the deadly gas leak at a pesticide plant in Bhophal, India, considered one of the world's worst industrial disasters. The incident involving Union Carbide India Limited, a subsidiary of Union Carbide, occurred in 1984. The death toll was never accurately determined but was in the thousands. Some of the deaths occurred at the time of the original leak, while others occurred later from gas-related diseases. Like the Shuttle disaster, there were warnings prior to the accident, including safety incidents, plant-management deficiencies involving unskilled workers and poor safety procedures.[12]

Dumb Ass people who do careless things or allow them to perpetuate can be harmful and even deadly. Although, in most cases, there are legal penalties and some level of restitution associated with these incidents, they do not begin to repay at a level commensurate with the losses and the pain caused by these disasters.

Dumb Asses in Staff Roles Are Out of Touch With Front-line Staff

Staff employees need to be well versed about the front-line people who deal with the customers, treat the patients, etc. People in staff functions who are oblivious to the demands of the front-line worker usually cause unnecessary work, tend to produce bureaucracy where it is not needed and generally make it difficult for front-line people to be effective.

An obvious problem with these people is that they have no appreciation for what it takes to deliver high-quality service or products to the customer. The out-of-touch people see only their very small piece of the enterprise. They work under the assumption that their work and product is of utmost importance, when the reality is quite different. Their sense of being revolves around trying to dictate to others in the organization what they have to do whether it makes any practical sense or not. They think nothing of making requests, often time-consuming, that detract from taking care of the customer. They become indignant when the requests are ignored or not fulfilled to their satisfaction. They are absolutely clueless about their real value within the organization.

Another breed of the "out of touch with reality" is the Dumb Ass known as the Bureaucrat on Steroids. These are the ones enamored with cumbersome processes rather than what is practical. They choose to be rule-oriented rather than flexible when the circumstances and common sense call for it. Most, if not all, organizations of any significant size have published policies, rules and procedures, but the bureaucrat will take them to nauseating extremes. The more rules and regulations, the more the Dumb Asses like it because they believe they don't have to use any judgment. Instead, they can simply hide behind policies and procedures. They worship policies and rules rather than being solution-oriented. If the situation is not covered by what is in writing, the Dumb Asses will try to make it fit. In other words, don't try to be logical with these people; it does not work.

Dumb Asses Tend to Reside at the Extremes of the Communication Spectrum

I have always maintained a healthy caution about people in the workplace who either never say anything or never shut up. The more important the role they play, the more cautious I get.

Let's start with the people who say nothing at all. First, a person who has nothing to say about anything begs the question, why are they employed? Regardless of the role, or how mundane the responsibilities, everyone should be, at some point, in a position to offer perspectives for the betterment of something in the organization. Even more confounding are people in leadership roles who don't communicate. How can anyone lead without communicating?

Some people are silent because they have worked in situations where employee input was not valued or a Barbarian boss may have shut them down. They don't speak because they have been conditioned not to take risks. However, if they don't get over their phobia, you have to question their value to the organization. Regarding these scenarios, I believe that it is reasonable to expect people to show sufficient resiliency—that, if given the opportunity, they will come out of their shell. Corporations require resilient people. People who are paralyzed by insecurity, bad experiences or lack of confidence should consider working in an environment other than a corporation (don't ask me where).

To not say anything at all is an extreme. Think of the people who, in most cases, have no problems at all expressing themselves, but when it involves a sensitive or critical situation, they shut down. More often than not, these are the people who want to get everyone else's perspective so they can assess which way the discussion and arguments are going before they commit. Under some circumstances, and depending on the person's position, you can argue that listening before committing is a wise strategy. Nevertheless, the person who uses this approach **all the time** is usually hunting for the right perspective or the politically correct one. People like this unfortunately tend to survive longer than the more extreme non-communicative group. They thrive in organizations that value group-think. However, they offer little, if anything, to organizations that value healthy discourse about the tough issues.

What about the incessant talkers? I cringe at the memories of the people who don't know when to shut up. These blabbermouths used to wear me out. Their first problem is that they don't listen. They only have one agenda: Their own. The organizational life expectancy for folks like this at the lower levels of the organization is not good. Unfortunately, some of them manage to sufficiently disguise their verbal diarrhea to make it into senior leadership positions, where they then run amok.

The incessant talker, especially those in high places, tends to also suffer from the malady known as self-centeredness. For a long time, it puzzled me that these people are so out of touch with how they are perceived. Eventually, I figured out that if they made it to a high level in the organization, these people simply don't care. I assume that, in their mind, they were rewarded for running off at the mouth, so they continue to yak away. Part of the mentality of these incessant talkers is that, in a perverse way, they love to listen to themselves. The value of what they say is often insignificant; it is more about having the podium and refusing to let it go. As a good friend of mine used to say, "They won't let go of the microphone."

It's been my experience that both Dumb Assess (and Egomaniacs, see Chapter Four), repeat themselves during their endless talking, but if a colleague even comes close to repeating themselves during a discussion or meeting, they are immediately called on it. This is the proverbial "Do as I Say, Not as I Do" syndrome. It is bad enough to be forced to put up with that type of behavior from a peer, but when it is someone at a higher level, it can be agonizing. With peers you can, at times, tune them out, but, with bosses, that is harder to do. These types of bosses expect everyone's undivided attention, regardless of their blatant duplicity.

More than once in my career, I worked with bosses or people more senior than me when I had to tolerate the incessant talking and the double standard. It made for arduous interactions and a quick loss of respect on my part for these people. My primary technique with these people was to consistently try to get them back on track. It didn't always work.

Dumb Asses Possess a Strong Sense of Entitlement

I learned early on that nothing is ever given in the corporate world. What you get must be earned, and it must be earned over and over again. Whether it's a raise, a promotion or a special assignment that recognizes your contributions, what you get must be won. To believe otherwise will usually lead to undesirable consequences. Regardless, many Dumb Asses act as if they are entitled. I have been amazed at some of the reasons people believe they are entitled. Some are incredibly trite, but real nonetheless. Among them are the following:

- Physically attractive people who are used to being the center of attention by receiving praise for their looks. Experts will tell you that physical traits matter in the corporate and political worlds. For example, if you are heavy or obese, there are people that claim you won't do as well climbing the corporate ladder. Taller people are often perceived as better leaders. There is something to that if you consider our presidents: Only 11 of the 44 presidents stood less than five feet nine inches tall. Since President Harry Truman, no president has been less than five feet 10 inches tall, and most have been six feet or taller.[13] Sadly, some people truly believe that their physical attributes somehow confer upon them privileges that are not available to the less attractive.

- People who believe they are smarter than everyone else. (There's more about these folks in the next chapter, devoted to the Egomaniacs.)

- People who believe that who they know is enough reason to be rewarded with promotions and other corporate privileges. This category is, unfortunately, not that uncommon. Time and time again, I experienced change at the top of a company or department where, within a relatively short period of time, the new leader would bring people to their organization with whom they had worked before. At face value, there is nothing wrong with this, particularly if the person being brought in is deserving of the position, and there are no capable incumbents. If there are worthy incumbents, then to summarily dismiss them sends a negative message to others in the organization. Accordingly, a new leader should at least get to know who is capable and who isn't before making wholesale changes in staff. You may argue that this view is a bit altruistic, but, in my view, it is certainly a better formula than pure cronyism. Most—and I wish I could say all—people who practice cronyism on a regular basis eventually learn that all they are doing is surrounding themselves with staff who think like they do, don't regularly challenge things that need to be confronted and eventually become so out of touch that it sinks them. There is much to be said for diversity of thought and backgrounds when it comes to success in the corporate world, especially in a global economy.

It is also important to note that many of the Dumb Asses who achieve success primarily because of who they know usually crash and burn when the crony leader is no longer in the picture.

- People who believe that because they have "paid the price" to reach a certain level in the organization, they can now be "retired on the job" and still expect to be rewarded or treated with a level of respect not commensurate with their current contributions. This one has always been particularly puzzling to me because in many cases it involves people who have worked very hard and achieved success, but at some point their perspective changed from continuing to do the things that got them to a high level to a belief that they are special.

A sub-category of this group is people who have been recognized with some prestigious award. Almost all the companies I worked for gave annual awards that recognized the top individuals within a department or the organization. As I look back in my career, I have lost count of the number of people who were recognized as "The Best of the Best" and at some point after the recognition were fired from the company. In most cases, if you analyze the reasons for their demise, you will find that people who were at one time Warriors somehow took a wrong turn and ended up Dumb Asses.

Success in corporations can be a fickle and fleeting thing. During my career, I went out of my way to coach those whom I mentored to never get too enamored with their achievements or recognition. It is certainly okay to be proud of special achievements and awards, but to think that they will result in unlimited career power is a big mistake. Instead, I believe that people should tackle each day as if yesterday's achievements did not matter. If trophies were involved as part of the recognition, my advice was to enjoy them for a day and then throw them in the closet. Bring them out when you retire and celebrate by boring your grandchildren about how great you were. Was this advice overly negative or curmudgeonly? Perhaps, but I believed strongly that it was certainly far better than believing that you are entitled. Most people have a very short memory when it comes to work. People expect leaders and co-workers to do what needs to be done today. What happened yesterday is just that… yesterday's news.

Will Rogers, actor, humorist and social commentator in the 1920s and 30s, profoundly described people who rest on their laurels by saying, "Even if you are on the right track, you will get run over if you just sit there."[14]

- Finally, there are people who came from a privileged background and think that the organization and its people need to continue to treat them in a manner commensurate with their social status. Some of these people are so out of touch with reality, it is amazing. Yet, think about it: A person born to money and a family with status in the community that had no one along the way to point out that they were not special, just fortunate, has no reason to expect that people in an organization will treat them differently from the manner to which they are accustomed.

Another version of this phenomenon are the people who graduate from an elite school and expect that this alone gives them special privileges. I'm grateful that I have never worked for an organization that valued where people graduated from more than what they could deliver. That said, there are many organizations where the school you graduated from makes a huge difference. Many law firms, and, to a lesser degree, accounting firms, are notable for such preferences. I have often wondered what it is like to be in one of these organizations and to find yourself dealing with paying customers who have no advanced degrees or graduated from Podunk University. It must be very unnerving for the Dumb Asses who graduated from "Prestige University" to cater to these mere mortals.

I worked for a family-owned business briefly during college and believe that most of them are great places to work, but I have heard plenty of horror stories from friends and family that make me cringe—specifically, organizations where undeserving, if not outright incompetent, family members hold key positions in the organization and abuse the privilege.

I'm grateful that in my career, my experience has been that people in almost all the above categories eventually get a dose of reality and either begin to earn what they get or crash and burn. Because it is a mindset that is not anchored to reality, the entitlement mentality is about as destructive a dynamic as I have experienced.

Dumb Asses Believe That There Are Certain Jobs or Tasks That Are Beneath Them

I strongly believe that, no matter what your role is, you should not be above doing any task that is a core component of the organization's product or services. Loading and unloading trucks can be backbreaking work, but almost every business receives or ships merchandise. Cleaning bathrooms in restaurants is not fun, but it is one of the primary things customers consider when judging the quality of the establishment. There are a myriad of hard and even unpleasant tasks on a manufacturing floor, but nothing gets produced if they don't get done.

I'm not suggesting that the Vice President of Finance needs to be in the restaurant cleaning toilets on a daily basis. But, if the situation presents itself, and if that person is in a restaurant during an unexpected set of circumstances and the toilets require cleaning, sleeves should be rolled up. To put oneself above such a task is basically insulting to the worker who regularly performs that job. You might as well be shouting, "What you do is menial and not important." Guess what: It does not get more important than these people, the ones who do the things that most people won't do. Try to survive without them.

You may argue that the situation with the VP is an extreme. I don't believe so, because this example goes to the core of what institutions are about and should not be taken lightly. In order for employees to feel pride and true commitment to an organization, its leaders are required to send the message that anything worth doing within the four walls of the enterprise is worth doing by everyone who receives a paycheck from the company.

A less extreme case involves the Dumb Asses who will go out of their way to pawn off unpleasant work on colleagues. This happens even when the task is core to the person's role, but they still avoid it or try to stick someone else with it. We have all worked with these people at one time. They are the ones who will run and hide when they see anything coming their way that they don't want to do. They go to great lengths to let someone else do it because they have "more important things to do."

The Dumb Asses who believe certain jobs are beneath them are well on their way to losing touch with the lifeblood of the enterprise. Moreover, they lose sight of a basic premise that all employees should ascribe to, which is how I can help the person taking care of the customer to be more efficient.

Prima Donnas are only important in operas. In the workplace, they set an unhealthy tone and hold teams back. If the person is a peer, be clear with him about how his behaviors are counter-productive. If it's the boss, ask for permission to provide input about how his actions may be perceived. If the boss does not grant permission or does not agree, focus on what you need to do. There is no upside to behaving poorly, even if your boss chooses to do so.

Dumb Asses Are Obsessed With Titles and Hierarchy

As organizations grow, the number of leadership levels and the number of people with fancy titles also increase. Dumb Asses are especially conscious of titles and perceived power. Some spend more time trying to get to know who is who in the organization than doing their job. If a vice president walks by, they put the kiss-butt mode in overdrive. At meetings they say what they think the highest-ranking person in the room wants to hear. At social events they hang all over the bosses like white on rice. What possesses people like this to think they can get by on just the adoration of the higher-ups is beyond me, but in my experience I have seen this behavior at all levels.

The amount of effort that some people put into these activities is mind-boggling. However, if you are an Egomaniac who loves the attention, you love to have Dumb Asses around admiring your every move and utterance. Have you ever been at a meeting talking to colleagues about an important issue without the boss or the big-title person in the room? Person A (the Dumb Ass) takes a position on some issue and goes to the point of talking down to a colleague who disagrees (Person B). Five minutes later, in comes the boss, who takes a position that is similar to the one expressed by Person B. Person A immediately changes his position and praises the boss for his enlightened insight. It would be laughable if it weren't so pathetic.

For people whose primary focus is to be noticed by the people at higher levels, there is no value proposition. Sure, they want to do things that will get them noticed, but they would rather spend more time on schmoozing and politicking than trying to get meaningful work done.

Dumb Asses Hear What They Want to Hear

With certain people it is impossible to reach agreement on some issues, so the best you can do is agree to disagree. To the extent possible on vital issues, you should also try to calibrate so that they understand your position. This is very difficult to do at times with people who are so into their position that they don't listen to alternatives or counterpoints. If they listen at all, it is to rebut, not to understand.

Worse yet are the people who only hear what they want to hear. Anything that is uncomfortable or disagreeable to them is automatically shut out or spun into something different than what was actually said. This can be very frustrating when it involves a colleague whose cooperation you need to get something done. If a subordinate is involved, it is somewhat less stressful but still frustrating. If a subordinate chooses to be obstinate, you can listen respectfully, but at some point, you have to end the discussion and move on. You can ask the subordinate to do what you need done, and they can decide to do it or face the consequences that are commensurate with refusing to follow the boss's request.

I abhor bureaucracy. One of the tenets of the bureaucratic mind is to document everything. I certainly don't support that. But with both situations just listed, documenting the discussion with the colleague or subordinate is sometimes the only effective way to get across to them. Specifically, both situations require a written follow-up with the person about what your position is on the issue and what you are asking the person to do.

There is a bigger problem if the situation involves a boss. At the end of the day, the boss is in charge, and, unless he puts you in a moral or legal dilemma, you need to do what you are being asked and, if necessary, seek perspective from a mentor or trusted colleague. I was fortunate in my career to find myself in relatively few situations where the boss consistently wasn't listening or only heard what he wanted to hear. I was, however, in these situations enough times to know that at some point the only alternative is to work on an exit strategy and find another job. I did it twice and don't regret either decision.

Dumb Asses Are Weak Strategic Thinkers

There is nothing more consternating and potentially dangerous for an organization than a leader at a senior level who does not think or act strategically. To not be a strategic thinker in many roles is limiting but not necessarily career ending or harmful to the organization—unless you are in a leadership role that can significantly impact the brand or the organization.

For senior leaders to lack a strategic mindset or perspective can result in adverse consequences. Most notably is not being able to see beyond the enterprise as it is today, both good and bad. It is the inability to study the internal and external trends impacting the organization and to be proactive rather than reactive. More importantly, it is being unable to study internal and external forces and moving people and resources in a direction that will optimize the organization's effectiveness and growth.

Lacking strategic mind-set often manifests itself in going back to solutions that are no longer effective. An example of someone suffering from this malady was the leader of one of the companies I worked at who, every time barriers were raised regarding a major issue impacting the organization, would resort to the same tired solution of, "We have to tackle better and harder." At some point you can tackle only so well, and new challenges require new solutions. Let me be clear: For a leader to occasionally suggest that people need to work harder is one thing, but to take that position consistently every time they are challenged is just Dumb Ass thinking. At some point people tune out. This person is a great example of what I said at the beginning of this book. Specifically, how many times have you asked yourself about someone in leadership, "How did this person ever get this high in the organization?"

One dynamic I have seen all too often is the person who steadily moves up the organization because they work hard and are loyal. In addition, somewhere along the line they have achieved some results. Working hard and being loyal are admirable traits, but they do not a leader make. The best engineer, nurse, machinist, or accountant is not guaranteed to be a great leader. Effective leaders need a strategic mindset.

"Executives need to be able to see around the corner.
Leadership is NOT about administration. Peter Drucker,

management consultant, educator and author said, 'Management is doing things right. Leadership is doing the right things.' I believe that Leadership is about defining reality and creating excitement and commitment for the future. Successful leaders need to be grounded in the reality of today and also be able to look around the corner in order to create a compelling future for the business and for anyone who has a stake in the business. Getting through barriers is not the ultimate gauge for a leader; avoiding the barriers is the real success. When a leader takes the time to think about and look around the corner, they can avoid barriers before they ever occur. Leaders who look around the corner can create a 'pull' for their vision as opposed to relying on a 'push' to force the vision through."

— STEVE RUSSELL, SENIOR VICE PRESIDENT, HUMAN RESOURCES, MCDONALD'S CORPORATION

Dumb Asses Make It Difficult for New People

There are certain Barbarians who like to make things difficult for new employees. If you are committed to the success of a company, then your focus is to look for opportunities to help make things better and more efficient. Dumb Asses take the opposite approach, especially when new people enter the organization. Rather than making new people feel welcome and valued, they treat them as if they have some rare contagious disease. Rather than helping with their training, they throw up unnecessary roadblocks. Whether it is insecurity that the new person will outperform them, or just being mean spirited, the results are the same, causing confusion and irritation for the new person.

This way of thinking is small-minded and defies logic, but many things and many people are not logical. I have found myself in this position more than once and learned the value of the adage, "Fool me once, shame on you; fool me twice, shame on me." Particularly when going into a new job, department or company, it is important to turn your people-assessment sensors on high alert to determine as quickly as possible who are the Warriors and who are the Dumb Asses. Then, as much as practical, steer clear of the latter.

It is easy when you are new to an organization to misjudge people at first meeting. Colleagues who may appear to be gregarious and congenial can turn into scorpions that will sting you. Some people may not make it difficult for the new person initially until the new person begins to perform at a high level and is accepted by other colleagues. That becomes the sign for the insecure or bitter individual to start making trouble for the new person. It's a sad situation for sure, but this happens in the best of organizations and at every level.

Working With the Dumb Asses

Dumb Asses reside at all levels. With any luck, your boss is not one of them, but if he or she is a Dumb Ass, you have a decision to make regarding enduring them or moving on to another role or organization.

If the Dumb Ass is a colleague, I know of no better way to endure them than by minimizing contact as much as is practical. Interact only to get the job done, and be polite, but avoid any activity not related to the job. Finally, and unfortunately, there is no expiration date on stupidity. As such, you must be constantly vigilant not to let your guard down and assume that the Dumb Asses will, somehow, begin acting like Warriors.

> *"The worst co-worker I ever had presented himself as a friend and was very interested in my particular area of expertise. He wanted to learn more, and I was willing to help him because his expertise complemented mine; there were things we could learn from each other. What I eventually learned was that, all along, he was plotting with my boss to take*

over my area and eliminate my role. Trust is a critical thing; bad co-workers abuse it."

— THOMAS E. KERESTES, FORMER GLOBAL COMMODITIES
MANAGER, BRITISH PETROLEUM CORPORATION

"Bad co-workers cause havoc and create more work for a high-performing team. If the statement 'a chain is only as strong as the weakest link' is true, then a bad co-worker is that weak link. These bad apples can come in many different types:

- *Non-performers*
- *Complainers*
- *Mediocre workers—the type who do just enough to get by*
- *Team disruptors—always questioning why, what, how, but they ask these questions only to disrupt, not to understand*
- *Individual player who doesn't support team goals*
- *Self-centered workers—in it only for themselves, sometimes to the point of 'glory-hogging' and only step up when there's something in it for them."*

— BUD LORD, DIRECTOR OF OPERATIONS,
MCDONALD'S CORPORATION

CHAPTER SUMMARY

Dumb Asses:

- *Rationalize failure and are blame-oriented*
- *In staff roles are out of touch with front-line staff*
- *Tend to reside at the extremes of the communication spectrum*
- *Possess a strong sense of entitlement*
- *Believe that there are certain jobs or tasks that are beneath them*

- *Are obsessed with titles and hierarchy*
- *Hear what they want to hear*
- *Are weak strategic thinkers*
- *Make it difficult for new people*

CHAPTER FOUR

The Egomaniacs

Like their fellow Barbarians, the Dumb Asses, Egomaniacs can be found at all levels of the organization. At the extreme, I tend to think of them as Egomaniacal Turds (see Bernie Madoff, page 72). With many of these people, it's not about the enterprise, it's about self-promotion, blind ambition and greed. Below are some of the common traits of these Barbarians.

Egomaniacs Believe That "It's All About Me"

At any level, Egomaniacs are the epitome of "dig me" and "I'm the center of the universe." When these narcissists are in high places in an organization, it can make for an unhealthy and dysfunctional workplace.

Here is an example: I had just arrived at a company and was out in the field talking to people about their jobs, their likes and dislikes. I was trying to learn about the culture that lay beyond the corporate headquarters. It was a Monday, and, throughout the day, I had sensed that people were uncomfortable and uneasy. At first, I thought it was me, since I was unknown to them and held a high-level position. However, as I went through the day, on four different occasions, I overheard some reference made to a certain university's football team losing over the past weekend and corresponding comments to the effect that it was going to be a long week. No one made these comments directly to me. Finally, I had to ask what it all meant. What I learned was that the vice president in charge of this territory was an alumnus of the university, and, whenever his team lost a football game, he would make life miserable for everyone.

Talk about "it's all about me!" Not only did he reveal serious maturity issues about not coping with the loss of a football game, he compounded the problem by taking it out on his subordinates. This VP was ultra critical of his people, threatened them and generally made life miserable for all around him until the funk of his team's loss wore off. It was a classic case of, "If I'm not happy, no one is happy." I thought I had heard the dumbest of the dumb workplace problems, but this one floored me. And it was not just dumb and egotistical; it was tragic that good, hard-working people would be forced to worry about going to their job just because of the outcome of a football game.

"My worst co-workers and bosses were people who were dishonest, controlling, manipulative, selfish and egotistical."
— ALMA ANGUIANO, DIRECTOR, ACCELERATED
OPERATIONS TRAINEE, MCDONALD'S CORPORATION

Another example of the "it is all about me" syndrome is the belief that there can never be enough self-congratulation. You know the type: They take credit for everything good that happens, whether or not they had anything to do with it. This is a sad thing for anyone to do at any level; for leaders to do it is especially pitiful. Specifically, these are leaders who take credit for the great ideas of their subordinates or assume credit for their excellent work. They give credit to no one and steal it whenever they see the opportunity. They covet the limelight but don't realize how poorly it reflects on them. They get so wrapped up in their self-importance they lose track of how shallow they have become.

Finally, when these "all about me" people choose to mix with the lowly peons in the organization, it is only to feed their egos. If a peon makes the mistake of trying to have a meaningful conversation, he or she is brushed off. What some of the poor, unsuspecting peons don't realize about these over-the-top narcissists is that it's all about appearances, not substance.

Egomaniacs Need People Who Flatter Them Fervently, aka Sycophants

This trait is a variation of the "it's all about me" mentality, but it is so important to the Egomaniacs it deserves its own category. This one is usually reserved for Egomaniacs at a leadership level. Specifically, this is the need that Egomaniacs have for an entourage of admirers. Another more common term for the admirers is "butt-kissers." They also exist in all organizations. These are the folks who follow the boss around and show their unflinching admiration at every opportunity. I've always thought that most of these people are so lacking in self-esteem that they adulate others as a means to feel that they are part of something important. That they pick Egomaniacs to admire seems to be lost on these sycophants, but I guess that is why they are so labeled. The Egomaniacs, in turn, value and need these people and the validation they offer.

One particularly pathetic version of this phenomenon is the expectation of Egomaniac leaders about subordinates remaining in the workplace until the leaders decide it is time to go home. If they feel like going for a drink or dinner after a long workday, subordinates are expected to be elated to join them. Both scenarios provide an opportunity for the Barbarian boss to orate about some meaningless topic that the sycophants will, undoubtedly, find incredibly interesting. Never mind that, for most people, the experience is akin to passing a kidney stone. What is interesting is that when these Barbarian bosses find themselves the last ones in the office or, with no one to follow them to the bar, they pout like spoiled babies.

I'm absolutely convinced that in large part the need of the Egomaniacal boss for sycophants is because they either have no personal life or a miserable one. Their only sense of worth and identity is in the job. They lose all semblance of balance between the personal and work life. As such, they build an insatiable need for an entourage at work to worship them. This, I believe, comes from pure selfishness. They lose track of the needs of those around them (co-workers and family) and put themselves into "it's all about me" over-drive. Sadder still is when someone points this out to the Egomaniac and they act as if they don't have a clue. They are so wrapped up in themselves they don't get that they are treating others as if their lives don't count. Sycophants play another role: As corporate "yes men" (and women), they validate, and never challenge, the Egomaniacs.

Perhaps the saddest thing about the sycophants is that many don't realize that, first, they are disposable and second, they put themselves in a high-risk position. They are disposable because while the Egomaniacal bosses expect loyalty from the sycophants, they don't give it. As long as the sycophant is convenient, the bosses support them, but if the actions of these admirers place the boss in a tough situation, they will be dumped in a heartbeat. That in itself is high risk, but the other way the sycophants are at high risk is when the Egomaniacal boss leaves the organization or goes down in flames. I have seen this happen time after time: As soon as the Egomaniacal boss is gone, companies find ways of also ensuring that the sycophants are history, too. The irony for the sycophants is that they don't realize that Egomaniacs hold an audacious disregard for those around them. The best that can be said about the sycophants is that some are gullible and are duped by strong personalities. Nonetheless, it makes you wonder: At what point does being gullible morph into being an imbecile?

> *"The worst boss I have ever had must have read every book on leadership management and, rather than take their advice, did exactly the opposite. This was even more disappointing*

considering that he is a graduate of one of the top management schools in the country!

"This 'gentleman' was arrogant and completely lacking in emotional intelligence. He was completely controlling and believed an organization should be run on the basis of fear. He expected undying loyalty simply because you had the honor of working for him. He did not trust or respect anyone but himself so was therefore unable to earn the trust and respect of anyone around him. He was the sole proprietor of the company and very intelligent but lacked the ability to relate to his employees and business partners. His completely self-absorbed nature and his lack of listening skills and common courtesy boggle the mind."

— GIL GOMEZ, ASSOCIATE PARTNER,
IBM GLOBAL BUSINESS SERVICES

Egomaniacs Are Indifferent About Harming Others

Egomaniacs do things that they perceive are good for them, often without regard to the harm they impose on others.

One of the most unforgettable professional experiences I had in my career was with the worst boss I ever had. This person made "good morning" sound more like an accusation than a greeting. He carried around every grudge he ever had and took great pleasure in trying to intimidate and demean anyone he could. If ever there was a disciple of "the beatings will continue until morale improves" approach to leadership, this guy was it.

I had reached the top position in Human Resources in this organization that was undergoing a change in leadership at the Chief Executive Officer/President level. The company was not growing at the level that the board of directors expected, and there were discussions about selling the company. When my boss did not move fast enough to fix things, the person described above replaced him. Though the new boss had been on our board of directors a short time, he did not know much about the company or its culture. Whatever he did know about the company, he did not seem to respect. For months I did everything I could to demonstrate to this Barbarian that I was a solid Human Resources Executive. There were two incidents with this guy that were both traumatic and, in retrospect, very valuable experiences.

The first incident occurred when the Barbarian boss asked me to lunch and told me that he was considering letting me go (aka firing me) but that he had been struggling with the decision because I had done everything he expected of me and more. Furthermore, he recognized that I was highly respected within the company. When I asked why letting me go was even an issue, the answer was: "I have worked with the same Human Resources Executive for the past twenty years. He is out of a job at present, and I want to bring him here." I was dumbfounded. I literally did not know what to say. When I regained my composure, I asked if I was being fired and the response was, "No, but I wanted you to know that I have thought about it and may still do it." Needless to say, after I came out of shock, I started applying for every job that made any sense at all. To my good fortune, weeks after my fateful meeting with the Barbarian boss, I found a great opportunity and took it.

The second incident started when I was still with the company but it did not play itself out until after I had left. About a month after the Barbarian CEO joined the company, one of the top financial people informed the CEO that he received an offer to work for another company and was resigning. The Barbarian CEO came to me and asked for help to make the finance person a counter offer because he could not afford to lose him. The CEO still needed to learn about the organization, and the financial person was important to that effort. Furthermore, since selling the company was in play, it was critical to retain this person's expertise. I helped with the preparation and communication of a counter offer. It was attractive enough that the financial person decided to turn down the new job offer and stay with the company. It was some months after I left that I heard the CEO had reached a point where he no longer needed the financial person's expertise and fired him.

When I heard about the financial person being fired, there were two thoughts that came to mind: First, I thought that was one of the most cold-blooded stories I had ever heard. Second, I realized how blessed I was to have put distance between that Barbarian CEO and myself.

Ironically, some of the best advice I ever received from anyone came from this Barbarian Boss, who said, "Much of our good judgment comes from our bad judgment." While he did not seem to learn much from his own mistakes and boorish behavior, he certainly repeated the phrase often enough. I learned a lot from that Barbarian, mostly about things I would never do.

Egomaniacs Believe That Only Their Ideas Have Merit

Smart leaders don't waste time reinventing the wheel. If something works, they adopt it. If the great idea came from another department or company, they try to learn as much about it and determine if it will work in their enterprise. Of course, not all great ideas are transferable from company to company. Differences in culture, talent and resources may make an idea unworkable in one enterprise while it will work very well in others. Still, Warrior Leaders don't summarily dismiss an idea because they or someone in their enterprise did not think of it. Instead, Warrior Leaders study great ideas and implement those that make sense for their environment. Egomaniacs, on the other hand, believe, "If it was not invented here, it has no merit."

The logic of "forget about learning from others—we will figure it out ourselves" is one of the most wasteful practices in any enterprise. People who think they have all the answers obstruct progress and creativity. They stifle learning and frustrate the people who believe there are often better ways to do things and to improve. When leaders stifle learning and new ideas, it is frustrating for people who are trying to improve the enterprise. Leaders who do not support ideas from outside their fiefdom are destined to discourage the open-minded and productive employees who will eventually find their way to a more productive environment.

Egomaniacs Combine Huge Egos With Insecurity

I have always found this dynamic to be fascinating, specifically, that the people who act like royalty are also the most insecure. Insecurity makes some people meek and lacking in self-esteem. It seems that, among the Egomaniacs, insecurity fuels their need to act superior even if deep inside they don't believe they are. They go around acting over-confident and in doing so make problems for themselves and those around them. You know what is said about confidence: It's that feeling you have before you fully understand the situation. Egomaniacs find themselves in that state time after time. When the light finally goes on, and they understand the situation, many over-react, creating chaos for those around them. The Egomaniacs fail to understand many situations because they come from the school of thought that declares, "When I want your opinion, I will give it to you." They also have problems with direct and honest people because Egomaniacs are so often untrustworthy themselves that they have difficulty believing anyone else. Trust, in general, is a foreign concept to most Egomaniacs.

One common way that the insecurity of Egomaniacal bosses plays out is through micro-managing people. The Egomaniacs need to control and to be the first to know about anything of any importance. As a result, they are constantly looking over their subordinates' shoulders and directing to the point where some subordinates do nothing unless they are told to do it. For most subordinates, this is irritating, and they spend more time trying to manage the Egomaniacal boss than doing actual work.

Then there are the Egomaniacs who are unsure about making key decisions. They become the masters of delay until they can figure out how it will impact them. Often times, they compound the indecision by hoarding information, but, if a subordinate obtains important information and does not tell the boss about it within nanoseconds, they will be, most likely, chastised for their gross indiscretion. Unreasonably delaying key decisions usually results in consternation for those who are impacted.

Finally, the insecurities of the Egomaniacs often manifest themselves in the need to be better or smarter than everyone else. If there is something I have learned over the years is that there are a ton of smart people in the corporate world, and the people who think they are smarter than everyone else are destined to learn they are only Dumb Asses with an ego. Warriors are comfortable with who they are. Colleagues, superiors or subordinates do not threaten them. The Egomaniac needs to feel superior, which often leads to surrounding themselves with people who they perceive are not as smart. Warriors take every opportunity they get to surround themselves with people who are better and smarter because they know it will invariably make them and the enterprise better.

The world is filled with smart people. For anyone to think they are smarter than everyone else is Egomaniacal with a truly dumb-ass state of mind.

> *"Really bad bosses were the extreme example of micro-managers who strangled creativity and leadership. It was 'their' way as the only way, and subordinates were measured by compliance, not creativity. This is the world that the kiss-ass thrives in, even if the overall business results fail to meet expectations."*
>
> — BRIAN UNGER, FORMER CHIEF OPERATING OFFICER, EINSTEIN NOAH RESTAURANT GROUP, INC.

Egomaniacs Often Feign Interest or Support

Enterprises require inter- and intra-departmental cooperation and collaboration to get many things done. If the work at hand is not important to the Egomaniac, he or she will often pretend to support it and then do nothing. Many use silence as their way of not challenging the value of what is being considered but at the same time not supporting it. Therefore, when dealing with the Egomaniac, it is important to either get them to commit or explain the reasons for their objections. The Egomaniac does not like to be called out in this manner, but better to suffer their scorn than to assume they will be supportive when they, in fact, have a different agenda.

Egomaniacs who believe they are smarter than everyone else will evaluate certain initiatives and convince themselves that "this, too, shall pass." They believe that by giving it lip service they can avoid any meaningful support. I, unfortunately, found myself in multiple situations throughout my career where it was clear to all involved that there were key people giving lip service or choosing the silent approach to avoid commitment to important initiatives. Lesson learned: the more important the issue, the more critical it is to ensure that the key players are committed to support the effort. Whenever I was leading an important initiative and sensed even a bit of passive resistance, I required each key player to go on record with their commitment to deliver what was expected of them.

Egomaniacs Shift Positions to Gain Favor

Egomaniacs are always on the lookout for anything that will make them look good, particularly in front of the boss. The corporate environment requires backbone, especially when you find yourself in contentious situations. To be obstinate about important issues, however, is not always wise. When the facts or counter-arguments to your position are persuasive, standing firm or ignoring the obvious will not help your case. The Egomaniac, on the other hand, will shift positions regardless of facts if they see it as an opportunity to gain favor with the boss or some other higher-up. They have no conviction about their positions, which results in everyone around them trying to guess what they will do next. They change for the sake of looking good rather than from thoughtful reflection. They change to appease and appear magnanimous rather than to support.

Egomaniacs Are Mostly Clueless About How Others Perceive Them

Did you ever find yourself in a situation where the Egomaniac trying to be humorous was anything but? Conversely, did you ever catch yourself trying not to laugh at something the Egomaniac thought was deadly serious? It is profoundly pitiful when people are so far into themselves that they are funny only when they are not trying to be. And how about the person who constantly follows up something they meant to be funny by saying, "That was a joke, people!" Clueless Egomaniacs do it on a regular basis.

There are Egomaniacs who can come across as very humorous, but their motives behind the humor are very different from that of Warrior Leaders. The Egomaniac uses humor as a way to say to all, "Look how great I am." The Warriors use it as a way to break the ice at a meeting or to be self-deprecating. You will seldom, if ever, find an Egomaniac being self-deprecating.

The advent of the 360 review, a feedback and development tool, has proven interesting for the Egomaniacs. The person being assessed receives input from several sources about their traits and behaviors. It requires the person being assessed to select a group of people, including the boss, peers and subordinates, who then provide confidential feedback via answers to a series of questions. These tools have been around a long time; I first became aware of them about 25 years ago. Boy, did I enjoy seeing the Egomaniacs get skewered the first time they were the subjects of a 360! Though the results are confidential and should be seen only by the person being assessed, it was evident from interacting with them that the Egomaniacs were not at all happy with the results (when Egomaniacs collide with reality, it can be very painful). Some Egomaniacs live in denial by not accepting the results. Others, being resourceful people, try to manipulate the results by selecting as many sycophants as possible to provide feedback. Funny what some people will do to avoid the truth. Finally there are some Egomaniacs who know exactly how they are perceived and simply don't care. They are in love with themselves, and that is good enough for them.

Egomaniacs Try to Define People

It is bad enough that most Egomaniacs don't get an accurate read on how they are perceived; some are driven to ensure that they are defining people they think they can influence. Specifically, they try to convince some people that they possess certain behaviors they need to change and others that they need to adopt. This is often done in the absence of any objective feedback about the person they are trying to influence. It is done merely because they want to have power over people. This is not coaching. It is an ego trip.

Usually when a person provides feedback to someone else, they are, in good conscience, trying to coach and assist. But before they can provide feedback, they either need to work with the person to make some direct judgments or solicit input about the individual from reliable sources. Egomaniacs don't bother with such specifics. They either provide perspective in a vacuum or seek only information that supports the balderdash they are trying to impart. By trying to exert their influence over the person, the Egomaniac is looking to self-aggrandize. To the novice receiving the input, this can result in confusion and, if the person is insecure, feelings of intimidation.

Here is an example: I received a call from a new HR director who had met with a vice president at our corporate headquarters. The purpose of their meeting was to get to know each other better. The new director had a dotted-line reporting relationship to me that required me to regularly provide him with developmental feedback. After the meeting with the vice president, the director told me he was confused. The development input received from the corporate VP was not consistent with the input he received from me. Naturally, he wanted to know what information I had given the corporate VP. My answer was none. I had not talked to the corporate VP at all about the new director. I then asked the director to share the input he had received; it was totally off the mark and without any basis in fact. When I confronted the corporate VP and asked where the information shared with the new director came from, they did what I would describe as the Michael Jackson "Backwards Moon Walk." The corporate VP had no reliable sources and had not solicited input from those who were in the best position to provide feedback. Had this been the only time I experienced this kind of behavior, I would have dismissed it as an aberration involving a self-absorbed VP. Unfortunately, I saw it happen time and again.

Egomaniacs Play the "Blame Game" When Things Go Wrong

Like their fellow Barbarians, the Dumb Asses, the Egomaniacs love the Blame Game. I once saw a plaque at a gift shop that read, "I did not say you were responsible, I said I was going to blame you." What a great way to describe the Blame Game characters. Egomaniacs will avoid responsibility for failure whenever they can get away with it, and, even when they can't, some will still try. The Egomaniac works from a presumption of guilt. When something goes wrong, they think, "Someone has to be guilty of something for this to have happened, and it is not going to be me."

"The two worst bosses I ever had possessed two fatal leadership flaws: no integrity and no character. They were abusive to me and other employees. Specifically, neither gentleman's word could be trusted. Time and time again, they promised

*something and either reneged or lied about having made
the commitment even though it was in writing. Making
other people squirm, especially their subordinates, allowed
their major shortfalls to be deflected so that they could not
be 'called out' on their prevarications."*

— DAVE THOMAS, FORMER CO-PRINCIPAL
AND OFFICER, LCA VISION

In the corporate world, the Blame Game may, at times, work in dysfunctional companies or departments, but, for the most part, it has a limited life span. It is limited because placing blame solves nothing; moreover, it alienates people. I've heard it said, and I believe it to be true, that "humiliation is a poor teacher."

Humiliation is what blame is all about. Blame seeks to demean, not to understand and fix. Companies that thrive are not blame oriented. They are solution oriented. Warrior Leaders don't dwell on failure, and they don't blame. They hold themselves and others accountable so that when things go wrong they can understand why and then focus on solutions. This is not to suggest that all corporations are pristine by any stretch of the imagination. However, at the end of the day, companies have to fix what went wrong, making restitution if it is warranted, or cease to exist. Unfortunately, and regardless of the remedies, sometimes people still get hurt, which is why the Egomaniacs and Dumb Asses can be so dangerous.

Egomaniacs Believe in Control Over Merit and Teach About the Values of the Organization but Don't Live Them

Egomaniacs cherish control. Achievement and merit are secondary to it. Egomaniacs know that to survive they need people who get results. But, if the achievers are not believers, rewards are few and far between. Merit takes a backseat to butt kissing.

Part of this dynamic is an inclination to be judgmental. Autocratic Egomaniacs believe themselves to be the judge and jury who will decide who is rewarded and who is punished. For those who are punished, discipline is not enough. They must also be belittled. The Egomaniac gets a thrill out of doing this. I have often thought that people who act this way were either beaten as children or repeatedly dropped in infancy. These are the same people who preach and lecture about the values of the organization, but, when it's convenient, they do not adhere to the values themselves.

Another nuance of the Autocratic Egomaniac is that they love to use fear as a way to control others. They give direction accompanied by warnings. They go something like this:

- "If you don't get this project done in time, there will be hell to pay."

- "If you don't meet the sales quota, you are done."

- "If you can't get your people to support this initiative, I'll get someone else who can."

If your boss is one of these fearmongers, it is probably time to explore working for someone else. Life is just too short.

Egomaniacs Act as if Only Their Time Is Important

The Egomaniacs exhibit a ravenous appetite for imposing themselves on others. An example of how this annoying habit plays out is the person who is constantly late for meetings but expects everyone else to be prompt. These Egomaniacs don't even have the decency to apologize when they are late. They act as if everyone should accept their chronic tardiness as a privilege bestowed upon them by a higher power. This is not only disrespectful but, more than anything, unproductive. Think of the time you have spent waiting for people who are constantly tardy to meetings and all the work you could have been doing while you were waiting for them to arrive. If several people are involved in a meeting and decide to start without the Egomaniac present, the Egomaniac, once he arrives, expects that the meeting be stopped until someone can recap everything that has been covered. This tendency to disregard the time of others is aggravating at best, but, when your boss is the culprit, it becomes more than that.

To manage this situation, two things are helpful. First, if at all practical, check with the boss's assistant to ascertain if he is running on time. If the boss is running late, ask the assistant to call when the boss is free. Second, if it is practical, bring along other work you can do while waiting for the boss to show up. Alternatively, you could tell the boss that, while you were waiting, other important work was not getting done. But let's be realistic—that would make too much sense, and the Egomaniacs don't much care about that.

"I worked with a CEO of a relatively small company ($10 million with 20 full-time employees) who read everyone's email. He would have our IT person blind copy him on every inbound and outbound email message that came through the company. He felt that was the only way he could know what was going on in the organization.

"He also expected all employees to keep track of their time and provide daily recaps of their activities in order to monitor 'progress.' He was the ultimate micro-manager and control freak. On top of all that, he would stroll in late every day and request meetings at random to fit 'his schedule.' He completely disregarded pre-arranged meetings, including those with customers. He would never communicate when he was going to be in the office, so the staff would never know

if he was available to speak to them or to a customer. He was a firm believer in 'Do what I say, not as I do.'"
— GIL GOMEZ, ASSOCIATE PARTNER,
IBM GLOBAL BUSINESS SERVICES

Egomaniacs Are Irrational about Hierarchy

While Dumb Asses are obsessed with hierarchy, the Egomaniac takes this obsession to a higher level of irrationality. Have you ever worked for someone who told you (note, I didn't say "asked") not to talk to their boss without letting them know first? Then do they demand to know what you wanted to talk with their boss about and why? There are also bosses who flat out tell you, "Never talk to my boss unless I tell you to do so." Anyone who demands to be in the loop if a person is going to have a discussion with someone above them in the hierarchy is at best a control freak and at worst has serious things to hide.

Let's be clear: I do believe in protocol and acknowledge there are things that should not be taken to higher levels without first addressing them with your boss. However, there are a myriad of things that are okay to discuss at a higher level without having to fear the wrath of said boss. An example is a chance meeting with the boss's superior in the hall or elevator, during which you are asked for your opinion on something. If it is something innocuous, you should feel free to respond. If it is something important that you have already discussed with your boss, you may also choose to respond. If, however, it is something important you have not yet covered with your boss, then say so to the higher-up and tell them you will follow up with your boss. There may be a scenario where something is asked that you and your boss disagree on. In that case, you should tell the higher-up that you'd rather have your boss follow up. If pushed by the higher-up as to why, be frank and say that you and your boss see the issue differently (without getting into the details). Also, whenever you discuss anything of consequence with a higher-up, you should always follow up with your boss to let him know what transpired.

These approaches are not on the level of rocket science; they are simply examples of professional courtesy and honesty. Yet, I was amazed by the number of times I was confronted by a boss who was bent out of shape because I had an innocent conversation with their boss. I also coached others who came to me for advice about how to handle a conversation they wanted to arrange with the boss's manager or how to deal with the fallout from one that had already taken place. The combination of egotism, insecurity and hierarchy can cause significant problems if not managed properly.

Turning the scenario around, there are Egomaniacs who believe it is beneath them to hold any meaningful conversation with anyone below them in the corporate hierarchy. If they want information from anyone at a lower level, they delegate the task to a subordinate. This practice often leads to the Egomaniacs losing touch with what is really happening throughout the business. If all the information you get from below a certain organizational level is filtered through someone else, you are bound to eventually get misleading, if not outright bad, information.

The truly off-the-wall Egomaniacs don't make it easy to communicate directly with anyone at, or below, their level. All such communication must be pre-arranged and flow through their assistant. Conversely, if anyone above the Egomaniac wants to discuss anything, however mundane, they jump through hoops to make themselves available. Anyone at a level higher than the Egomaniac's gets unfettered access to them. Everyone else gets in line and hopes the Egomaniac's assistant likes them.

One of the most disappointing things I experienced throughout my career was to see Warriors turn into Egomaniacs. These were people who did all the right things, in the right way, to get to a certain level only to turn into a Barbarian. As people rise through organizations, they should keep reminding themselves where they came from (which, in many cases, is a humble beginning). Unfortunately, some folks lose track of where they came from. Others conveniently forget about all the people who helped and supported them along the way. Below are some ways in which this scenario plays out:

- The people who helped the Nouveau Barbarian achieve success are no longer important. Therefore, they are ignored, if not totally forgotten, both at, and away from, work. Socializing with the unimportant becomes taboo.

- Old convictions and observations about the business are ditched if the Nouveau Barbarian believes that they could be considered controversial and therefore shed a questionable light on the Barbarian's newly acquired status.

- While before he achieved lofty status, the Nouveau Barbarian was willing to challenge the status quo, he is now a firm supporter of the same, particularly if he sees that doing so gives him an advantage with his superiors.

- Where before they shared information for the sake of the enterprise, Nouveau Barbarians now hoard it for selfish reasons.

Tips on Working With the Egomaniacs

First, identify the Egomaniac. This is not too hard since Egomaniacs make it clear to the entire world that they are better than everyone else and that, wherever they roam, they are deserving of everyone's full attention and admiration.

When dealing with the Egomaniac on important issues, it is always good to know what is in it for them. They may try to disguise their motives, but know that, more often than not, they are looking for an angle that will benefit them in some way. Find out what that is, and you'll have greater control in your interactions with them.

That is not to suggest that you must agree with them on everything, which is exactly what they want you to do. It is to say that knowing what they want can help you manage the course of a discussion and avoid obvious disagreement or conflict. However, there will be times when it is necessary that you be very clear about what your position is, regardless of where the Egomaniac stands.

Knowing what the Egomaniac wants may also be advantageous by allowing them to take credit for something of importance to them. As long as it does not compromise you or others, let them take the credit. If, on the other hand, letting them take the credit compromises you or other colleagues, then there is no choice but to face the Egomaniac head-on. Do it professionally, but do it. Unfortunately (or fortunately, as the case may be), there is no reconciliation with the Egomaniac. You will lose favor with them when they are challenged, but you will most likely be in very good company.

Finally, it is easy to allow Egomaniacs to upset and rattle you with their toxic behaviors. Be conscious not to let their ways steer you into doing Dumb Ass things. The best way to deal with the Egomaniacs is to follow the same advice about Dumb Asses: Avoid them whenever and wherever practical.

CHAPTER SUMMARY

Egomaniacs:

- *Believe that "it's all about me"*
- *Need people who flatter them fervently, aka sycophants*
- *Are indifferent about harming others*
- *Believe that only their ideas have merit*
- *Combine huge egos with insecurity*
- *Often feign interest or support*
- *Shift positions to gain favor*

- *Are mostly clueless about how others perceive them*
- *Try to define people*
- *Play the "Blame Game" when things go wrong*
- *Believe in control over merit and teach about the values of the organization but don't live them*
- *Act as if only their time is important*
- *Are irrational about hierarchy*

CHAPTER FIVE

Mentors

Throughout the first four chapters, I used qualifying words like "some," "at times," "many" and "others" to describe Warriors and Barbarians. Doing so recognizes that relatively few people possess all the traits I attributed to the Warriors and, thankfully, few reveal all the traits belonging to the Barbarians. The reality is that most of us behave in ways that place us somewhere along the spectrum that runs between the two. I like to think that most of us are moving toward the Warrior end of the spectrum but, as we know all too well, some people will invariably be drawn in the direction of the Barbarians. Where you find yourself on the spectrum can depend, in large part, on your mentors.

All of us need people to help us along the way, for the whole way. What we do, the roles we play and the colleagues we work with are constantly changing. These changes are sometimes for the good, and sometimes not. That is why the role of mentors is so important. Their judgment can be a valuable guide, as well as provide sound counsel throughout your journeys in the corporate world.

> *"Once I learned the difference between a mentor and an advocate, I was able to make better choices about whom to ask for help. Advocates are great for support on something*

113

specific, but mentors, in addition to supporting specific things, are broader and act as tutors. My best mentors let me know, in an honest and caring way, what I needed to do to improve my skills and visibility. They were people I could count on to give me the 'word' on what was being said about me. They were also willing to tell me what I needed to hear, even though it may have been painful. Finally, they recommended me for projects and high-visibility teams that helped my career"

— Cody Teets, Vice President and General Manager, McDonald's Corporation

Mentors are significant for a myriad of reasons, among them that they:

- Help you to see and recognize important aspects of the organization that may not be readily apparent, for example, the culture and nuances of leadership
- Aid you to understand the stated and unstated values of the organization (also part of the culture)
- Steer you through challenging times by coaching about potential courses of action
- Show how to put good and bad experiences into perspective
- Help you to effectively manage the Barbarians
- Provide support with other leaders in the organization
- Offer perspective on skills you need to develop and those you need to improve
- Provide insight on important career decisions

The formal term for the experienced person who guides and coaches a less-experienced person is the mentor. The person seeking guidance is often referred to as the protégé. The origin of the word protégé is French and means "to protect." For our purposes, it means a person under the patronage, protection or guidance of someone interested in his or her career or professional growth (the Mentor).

There have been books written about how to be a good mentor and protégé and how to have a productive relationship. Some companies provide online mentor/protégé matching sites. In my opinion, the mentor/protégé relationship should be relatively simple, but like so many other things in corporations, some make the mentor/protégé concept overcomplicated. Basically, you can use common sense to figure out whom you should rely on for help and perspective and how to make the relationship a success.

> *"I valued my mentors because they told me the truth and they were not afraid of hurting my feelings. They cared about me as an employee and a person. I continued to get better as a person because of the people who have been my mentors."*
> — VICKI GUSTER-HINES, REGIONAL VICE PRESIDENT OF OPERATIONS, MCDONALD'S CORPORATION

Protégés

- I believe that 95 percent of the responsibility to make a mentor/protégé relationship successful lies with the protégé. If the protégé truly wants to learn and receive coaching from a more senior person, then he or she must be responsible and assertive about arranging time with the mentor.

- The protégé has to be open to learning from the mentor, including receiving constructive criticism. This, after all, is the primary value of a mentor. However, the protégé must also be cognizant that mentors are not always right, nor do they always give the best advice. Because you admire and trust someone does not render that person infallible. Accordingly, it is wise for the protégé to seek more than one mentor.

- Protégés should seek mentors both within and outside their organization. They should also look for mentors in different functional disciplines. The broader the source of perspectives, the more opportunity there is to gain a better overall understanding of the important issues.

"I believe there is a mentor for every stage of someone's life and career and that mentors should not be limited to your area of expertise, function or company. The more diverse your mentor base is, the better.

"Regarding the relationship with your mentor, you have to put forth the effort to make it worthwhile. When both the mentor and the protégé walk away feeling that each has had a positive impact on the other, that is when you know that you've had a successful relationship."

— ALMA ANGUIANO, DIRECTOR, ACCELERATED
OPERATIONS TRAINEE, McDONALD'S CORPORATION

- In choosing a mentor, the protégé should pursue individuals they respect, who achieved significant experience in business and, preferably, hold positions that are two or more levels higher up the ladder. The protégé must also recognize that position and/or years of experience of and by themselves do not necessarily qualify someone to be a good mentor.

- In addition to mentors, the protégé should identify trusted colleagues at their level and below. These people may not have the same depth of experience as a mentor, but they can provide invaluable perspective on a wide range of issues. These should be people who are successful, trustworthy and reliable.

- Finally, a protégé should not reach out to a mentor or colleagues only when there is a problem. The protégé needs to remember that this is a relationship. Accordingly, reaching out only when there is a problem or when you are in panic mode does not develop the best foundation on which to build a relationship. Regular and consistent contact, regardless of whether times are good or bad, is a much healthier way to build and maintain the relationship.

Mentors

- A good mentor will get to know the protégé, including understanding the person's strengths, weaknesses and career aspirations.

- A good mentor should not attempt to provide perspectives on issues outside their areas of expertise. If the protégé seeks input on such issues, the best advice the mentor can give is to refer the protégé to another, better source.

- A good mentor will do his or her best to be accessible to the protégé and provide guidelines about how and when they prefer to be contacted. A mentor has to be willing to make time for the protégé; if they cannot, they should be honest and tell the protégé that their time is limited or that they need to end the relationship. It may be harsh, but the reality is that just because a protégé seeks counsel, it does not make them worthy of the mentor's time and effort.

- A good mentor will be brutally honest with a protégé but always in a constructive manner.

- If the mentor works in the same organization as the protégé, the advisor will ensure that things discussed in confidence remain that way.

- A good mentor will recognize that getting too close with a protégé may not be the wisest course. Knowing a person well and being too familiar are two different things. Being too familiar can result in the mentor not being as objective and honest as they need to be. It can taint the mentor's perspective about the protégé and result in poor coaching.

I have known several people over the years who could, technically, have been considered mentors of mine. Likewise, I knew people who might be considered my protégés. I don't recall ever asking anyone to be my mentor. Nor do I remember any protégés ever formally asking me to be their mentor. Instead these relationships simply evolved over time. If I met someone I thought could help me, I would ask if it was okay to contact him from time to time to get his perspective on things. That is how all of my so-called mentor/protégé relationships started. And while I did not know it at the time, this informal approach saved me from some potentially embarrassing and frustrating situations. While I was right about most people I chose to contact, in a few cases I soon realized that some people I thought were in the Warrior category were closer to the Barbarian end of the spectrum. Because I had not gone as far as to establish a formal mentor/protégé relationship with these people, I could simply hang up the phone and never call again.

As regards the people who reached out to me, if I did not know them well, I would spend the initial meeting or meetings trying to get to know them and how they viewed themselves and those around them. Some of these people were not individuals I wanted to spend time with, as their tendencies were clearly to the far end of the Barbarian spectrum. My approach in these situations was to not encourage further meetings. If that did not work, I was direct and suggested they seek someone else for perspective. Those conversations were not always pleasant, but at least it stopped us from wasting time—theirs and mine.

Asking a person that you don't know well to be your mentor or, conversely, being asked by someone you don't know to be a mentor can cause the relationship to be concluded more quickly than it should. If this sounds like what couples go through, it is quite similar. Get to know each other before making a commitment you might later regret. If you know the person well, establishing a mentor/protégé relationship is much easier. Ask if you can call them from time to time for advice and perspective, and you should be on your way.

> *"My best mentor was my first sales manager, with whom I still talk today. He 'walked the talk' in its truest sense and was always there for me during good times and bad times."*
> — Thomas E. Kerestes, Former Global Commodities Manager, British Petroleum Corporation

> *"My best mentor showed he cared about me as a person. He helped improve my analytical and strategic skills and has always shown me respect. He encouraged me to continue to grow. His coaching and perspective gave me the necessary confidence to succeed. He's also been a key advocate in my career advancement."*
> — Kim Bayer, Division Marketing Officer, McDonald's Corporation

Mentors can be instrumental in helping you navigate the morass that corporations can sometimes be. As important, they can offer invaluable perspective on career opportunities and growth. Though entering into a mentor/protégé relationship is a significant and sensitive matter, it does not have to be arduous. Focus on people you respect, and keep it simple.

CHAPTER SIX

The Good, the Bad and the Ugly of Key Departments

Just like Warriors and Barbarians, functional departments within an organization also possess good and not-so-good traits. Why? Because departments are populated by people who shape the culture and personality of the department. Moreover, the leadership of each department has the greatest impact in shaping its culture. At some level, we are all a reflection of the people we work for, good or bad. As such, some departments will take on the Warrior traits, while others will gravitate toward the Barbarian traits. I'm not suggesting that if the leader of a department tends to be a Barbarian that all the employees in that department are the same. However, departments gain a reputation, just as individuals do.

Unfortunately, those outside of a company or department just looking in tend to paint people with a wide brush. By way of example, over the past few years, there have been significant increases in gas prices. In 2012 I was on a road trip through California where I paid almost five dollars per gallon. That is a price level that was unimaginable to most people a few years ago, even though the experts were telling us that it could happen. What do we hear on the news about gas prices? That the oil companies are trying to gouge us; that the oil companies should not get any tax breaks because they are making too much money as it is; that, while the perception is that prices go up overnight when something adversely affecting supply occurs, when something favorable occurs, it takes forever for prices to come down, etc. Be honest: what is your perception of oil companies when you hear all these indictments? Also, what is your perception of people who work for oil companies? Are they all Barbarians? I don't believe so.

Like individuals, departments function somewhere between the Warrior and Barbarian ends of the spectrum. Generally speaking, the characteristics of departments that function at the Warrior end of the spectrum and Warrior Leaders at the Helm tend to:

- Understand the business and the industry, not just their discipline
- Recognize who the paying customers are and what they value
- Appreciate their role in the organization and don't act as if they are the center of the universe
- Realize what it takes for the entire business to succeed and not just their function
- Think and act cooperatively, rather than unilaterally, with other departments
- Communicate in a manner that makes sense for people in other departments. Most important, they translate their technical nuances and lexicon into plain English.
- Focus on making things simple for people and eliminate bureaucracy whenever practical
- Be respectful of the pressures of other departments
- Continually work to improve their overall level of competence

- Actively support the goals and strategies of the company, including making adjustments in resources when necessary to optimize that support
- Concentrate on the "Art of the Possible" rather than rationalizing failure
- Set high standards for themselves and their function
- Think in terms of team rather than self. This mindset applies to interactions within the department as well as with other departments.
- Hold themselves accountable
- Have a sense of urgency about getting things done
- View other departments as customers, not competitors
- Anticipate customer needs and help to address them
- Are flexible and adaptable to help tackle the changing demands on the business. This includes scheduling major activities in a way that is congruent with the cycles of the business.
- Make it fun for those around them as well as themselves

Conversely, the characteristics of departments that are led by Barbarians tend to:

- Revel in the nuances of their discipline but don't always understand the overall business
- Forget, at times, that paying customers exist, or even consider them to be a nuisance
- Believe theirs is the most important function and all other disciplines are inferior. Some try to dictate to other departments.
- Are certain that if only they succeed, everyone else in the business succeeds as well
- Think nothing of making decisions in a vacuum. After all, they know best.

- Speak in the technical lexicon of their function and expect others to learn it. Those who don't are talked down to as if they don't possess a single brain cell.
- Do not understand when people from other departments react adversely to complex and unrealistic expectations or processes
- Are disrespectful of the pressures faced by people in other functions
- Believe if they are technically competent, that is enough. Communication skills, leadership, etc., are not a priority.
- Are very centric in how they view the business. They believe that department strategies and goals, rather than the overall health of the company, are the most critical factors.
- Are inclined to rationalize their own failures while having no tolerance for the failures of others
- Believe that they, and their discipline, are the pinnacle of knowledge and look down on other disciplines
- Hold everyone but himself or herself accountable
- Believe that theirs is the most important function and that others must follow their lead
- Believe that anything they need from others must be addressed yesterday. However, anything anyone else needs must be prioritized, if not ignored.
- Do not understand, much less value, the concept of internal customers
- React to change only when forced to do so

Once again, I will offer a disclaimer. No department in any discipline that I ever knew functioned solely at the Warrior end of the spectrum. Even Warrior-led departments include opportunities for improvement. Conversely, if any department functioned solely at the Barbarian end of the spectrum as I have described, it would implode.

Many unfortunate activities invariably occur in departments that are at the Barbarian end of the spectrum. These activities have consequences. One consequence is that the people in the department become so insular that they lose touch with the business and begin to believe they are infallible. When an individual, a functional department or a company shuts out those around them (especially the customer), and begins to listen only to himself or herself, unfortunate, if not catastrophic, things begin to happen.

Here are some perspectives on a handful of major departments and the things that have stuck with me throughout the years.

- Human Resources, or HR, is a term that was not widely used until the late '80s. Previously, the function was called Personnel and in most companies, it was largely administrative. In the early years of my career, it was interesting to me that Human Resources was at its strongest and showed its greatest influence in companies that had unions. The reason was simple: somebody had to negotiate contracts, deal with arbitrations and manage the daily challenges a union can create between management and employees. Not surprisingly, the HR function in those companies played a key role in the success or failure of the enterprise.

At a very high level, as unions waned and the general workforce became more diverse, the importance of the HR function in leading companies shifted more toward workforce planning, including the development and retention of key talent. Over the years the design and management of benefit and compensation programs became increasingly more complex and, as a result, HR professionals became more prominent. In addition, the increasing amount of workplace legislation has made it more challenging for leaders across all functions to manage people. As such, HR has taken the role to ensure corporate compliance. More importantly, to my mind, is the role that HR plays in ensuring that the enterprise has the necessary people resources to stay competitive in an increasingly complex world.

Some HR folks suffer from forgetting they work in a business and not a social agency. To be effective, it is important for HR professionals to have the skill and desire to work with people. It is as important that the HR professional be an advocate for good leadership and people practices. HR professionals can, however, cross the line into ineffectiveness when they are all about people without regard to—and in extreme cases, in spite of—the business. I have always felt strongly that for any HR person to be effective, he or she first must be a solid business person. If you can't position what you are arguing for in the context of the business, then you have lost the battle. Great people practices need to be founded on the business of the business. When recommendations by HR professionals are not founded on the business, they will, at best, be given lip service and, at worst, will be ignored. "I love working with people" by and of itself, doesn't cut it.

- **Accounting/Finance:**

The accounting function can be either a blessing or a drag on most businesses. Accounting and Finance departments that can provide advice to leadership based on sound analysis absent the histrionics are invaluable. Those that resort to scare tactics and the "cut costs to the bone" mentality when the business experiences a down-cycle can be harmful.

I once worked with a chief financial officer who, every time he was unhappy with sales for a given period, would always use the same line: "We are hemorrhaging money." It did not help that this guy, in my opinion, also had the social skills of a Yeti. All businesses go through cycles, with some relying on a few months of the year to make most of their operating income. Consequently, there will be times when sales and income are not going to be the best, but this does not necessarily translate into a catastrophe.

I worked in companies that were sold to the new owners who cut cost to the point that it was difficult to open for business. I worked in companies that went into slashing-cost mode at the mildest sign of a sales downturn. I also worked for companies where spending was out of control. While I don't know of many businesses that consistently spend like drunken sailors and succeeded, neither do I know of many businesses that cut costs into growth and prosperity.

As with most things in business, the important thing is to find the right balance. Accounting staff is critical to ensuring that the business finds proper balance. To do so, they need to have a handle on the numbers as well as an understanding of, and an intuition for, the business, the industry and its nuances.

I had the privilege of working with accounting leaders who did not mince words when it came to identifying financial concerns about the business but, like all great leaders, were not shortsighted. They maintained the ability to look ahead and put the current concerns in their proper place. More importantly, they made recommendations that were practical and sensible for both the short-term reality and the long-term prospects of the business.

- **Marketing:**

  Marketing departments can create excitement about the products and services of a company and energize its employees. They can also generate, among customers and employees, a pride in and a sense of connection to their products. On the other hand, when they lose touch with the customer or the reality of the business, they can produce confusion for the customers and havoc for employees. Take, for example, a marketing campaign that is difficult or confusing for employees to execute. If the employees who interact with the customer either don't get it or are not excited about it, then there is very little chance that the customer will be, either.

- **Legal:**

  In my years in the corporate arena, most of my experiences with attorneys were with Labor Legal Specialists. There are many other legal specialties, and I suspect that some of what I'll cover about labor attorneys also applies to them.

  At the start, it is important to recognize that whatever the issue, a good attorney wants to win her case. Corporate attorneys have the added burden of protecting the brand they represent. Therefore, they carry a heavy load, especially when the Dumb Asses are out and about doing stupid stuff that gets companies in legal trouble. Regrettably, this occurs more frequently than the attorneys would like.

  The Warrior corporate attorneys are first and foremost proactive. They don't wait for things to go wrong; instead, they try to educate their constituents in order to avoid legal entanglements. The Warrior attorneys stay close to the business and proactively identify areas of potential concern. They have the wisdom to review each case not just within the legal parameters of the situation but also in the broader context of the business.

By this I mean that they take into account the harm that may be inflicted on the business instead of always holding out for a defensible, airtight case. An example that I was involved with all too often is one in which a manager wants to terminate a troublesome employee. The employee may be a menace to the people around him and a hindrance to the effectiveness of the work group, but there is not sufficient documentation or corroboration regarding the employee's poor behavior to make it a clear-cut defensible case. Many of the managers involved in these situations have clearly not done their job. They may have tolerated the employee's behavior, or they may have talked to the employee or even issued a reprimand but failed to document it. In any case, although it may be legally risky to fire the employee, the Warrior attorney will weigh that risk against the continued presence of the employee in the work environment and its adverse consequences.

On the other hand, Barbarian attorneys will not support terminations or any disciplinary actions regarding troublesome employees until each legal "i" has been dotted and every "t" has been crossed. They try to impose legal arguments and safeguards to impractical levels. These attorneys have no appreciation about the adverse impact that poor or boorish employees can have on a work team and, by extension, on the business. Some try to dictate legal requirements that can reach a point of absurdity. Their sole goal is a 100 percent defensible legal case. I worked with some attorneys I accused of wanting to kill a mosquito with a bazooka. The lengths to which they wanted managers to go for a strong legal case were not only impractical, they were overkill. Though not something that should be condoned, some managers give up and work around poor employees rather than take all the steps that the overzealous attorney would demand.

Warrior attorneys can be your best and most valuable colleagues. They not only steer you in the right direction regarding challenging and contentious situations, they can also save your butt when you did not do a proper job handling a legally risky situation. Barbarian attorneys, on the other hand, can be pedantic, obstructive and unrealistic.

- **Operations:**

    The term "Operations," as I use it throughout this book, refers to those employees in an enterprise who are closest to the customer. In some companies, Operations consists of the sales force; in others, it is the people who make the products (or deliver the services); and still, in others, it is the employees who do both. Without Operations, there are no products or services. All other functions in the company support Operations to varying degrees. All those other functions will, at some time or another, ask Operations staff to perform fiduciary duties that are related to expected business processes or legal compliance.

    The great Operations Teams focus on the customer and rely on the expertise of the staff functions to improve their effectiveness. Sound Operations people know and value that it takes a team of competent line staff and functional Subject Matter Experts to optimize the effectiveness of the corporation. They also help the people in the support functions to get a better understanding of the products and services they deliver and, most of all, to understand the customer.

The not-so-great Operations Teams believe that support functions should be allowed into their inner sanctum only when they need something. They believe that employees who perform support functions are second-class citizens and treat them as if they are basically a collection of troublesome mutants. In this day and age, if only from a compliance perspective, this belief system is a train wreck waiting to happen. If not across an entire company, there are pockets of Operations staff or leaders who have no appreciation for anyone in a support role. Regardless of how widespread this mindset might be in a company, this way of thinking is dangerous to the brand and obviously discouraging for support staff.

Depending on the size of the company and the industry, there may be other departments in the enterprise like Communications, Training, Public Relations, Government Relations and others. These departments, like the ones discussed, can be either a vital part of the business or a drag on the business, depending on where they operate on the Warrior/Barbarian spectrum.

> *"Based on my experience there are several characteristics of successful and highly respected functional departments within an organization. To begin, it is crucial that the leader of the functional department be a respected and integral part of the Senior Management team. Among a myriad of responsibilities, this leader establishes the vision and mission for the functional department and ensures that they are key drivers of the company's success. This strategic linkage between the functional department and the organization helps set the function up for success. Another key characteristic of highly effective functions centers on the ability of the team members of the function to establish and maintain a strong trust with the rest of the organization. To truly establish trust,*

the team members must be perceived as reliable, open to feedback and input, competent (true subject matter experts in their area of expertise) and have high integrity. All four areas must exist for a trusting relationship. Trust takes hard work and time to build."

— Steve Russell, Senior Vice President, Human Resources, McDonald's Corporation

Competent managers are important to ensure proper execution, but departments, like companies, still require strong leadership to ensure lasting success

CHAPTER SEVEN

The Lunacy of Corporate Speak

Corporations are complex organizations with lots of moving parts. Dealing with Barbarians and their challenging behaviors adds to the complexity. Layer on top of that a confusing lexicon, and navigating the corporate arena can, at times, become daunting.

I was born in Cuba and immigrated to the US with my brother in 1962. I was nine years old, and neither my brother nor I spoke a word of English. Our parents stayed behind in Cuba, so the only Spanish-speaking person we knew was our great aunt, who committed to watch over us until our parents could join us. When we first arrived in America, like thousands of other Cubans before and after us, we spent two weeks in Miami. With so many Cubans around us, speaking English was not that critical. Then my great aunt informed us that we were moving to Memphis, Tennessee. Call me crazy, and I did not research this, but I don't believe there were many Spanish-speaking people in Memphis in 1962. Accordingly, my brother and I went through a "baptism by fire" to learn the English language. No one in the school we attended or the apartments we lived in spoke Spanish. No matter where we went, no one spoke Spanish. To compound matters, we had no TV, so trying to pick up some of the language through that medium was not an option.

To help our immersion into the new language, my aunt spoke to us in English as much as possible. We stayed after school every day, and one of the nuns spent time teaching us the language. After about eight months, my mom and dad where able to join us and we ended up in Chicago, where my dad found employment. There were a few more Spanish-speaking people in Chicago than there were in Memphis, but not many.

I remember an old and rather lame joke that many Cubans told when coming to the States that speaks to the total confusion people could experience when they are new to a country where they do not know the language. The story is that a Cuban is lost and can't find his way back home. He is standing at an intersection and finds a phone booth. He calls his friend to ask if he can come get him and take him home. The accommodating friend says, "Of course, I'll come get you. Look at the street signs and tell me where you are." The lost Cuban looks up and tells his friend that he is at the corner of "One Way and Don't Walk." While slightly amusing, this experience was not far from the reality of what non-native speaking people encounter in a new country.

Another perspective regarding this topic is important. I have travelled abroad to several non-English-speaking countries. Whether on business or vacation, I may have experienced some temporary difficulties, but because my time in these countries was limited, not knowing the language caused only minor inconveniences. When you are in a country where you are going to live, however, learning the new language becomes vital to your survival.

Every country has its idioms, slang and catch phrases. Depending on where you live in the U.S., you may hear different idioms. Imagine that you don't speak a word of English, and, not only are you forced to learn the language, you also need to decipher slang. Trust me: this can be both interesting and confusing. By way of example, consider the idiomatic phrase "cut it out." In English it means asking someone to stop talking or doing something that, in some cases, may be annoying. Then there is "knock it off," which means exactly the same thing. From the time I was nine until I was almost out of high school, I had a mental block about these two phrases and would confuse them. Instead of saying, "cut it out," I would say, "cut it off," and instead of "knock it off," I would say, "knock it out."

Within this context, Corporate Speak is found in a variety of forms. The most common and potentially confusing is the use of sports idioms or other catchphrases applied to corporate issues. "Spinning" information and being overly politically correct can also cause corporate environments to be more challenging and confusing than they need to be.

Confusing Terms, Idioms and Catchphrases

Everyday idioms, catchphrases and misleading terms can be confusing and difficult to decipher within the context of conducting business.

There are idioms that people use in everyday life that also creep into the corporate world. While confusing, these phrases are relatively harmless in everyday life. However, in the corporate environment, they become more important because, in many cases, they require an appropriate response. Though not all people who use these phrases should be considered Barbarians, you have to wonder about those who use them all the time. Let's explore a few.

Everyday-life idioms and familiar phrases used in business settings:

- I always thought that "full" meant "full," "empty" meant "empty," and so on. How many times have you been on a plane and the flight attendant comes over the intercom and announces, ***"We have a very full flight today."*** The flight is either full, or it is not. If it were not full, I would prefer an announcement that is more accurate, such as: "There are only five empty seats on this flight." As much time as I spent on planes, even the smallest of improvements regarding clarity was important to me.

- He or she has their *"ducks in a row."* I think this means that everything is in order or ready to go. I have heard this one used so many different ways that I'm not sure there is a common understanding of what it is supposed to mean.

- That *"does not cut the mustard."* This usually means that something is not acceptable. Did you ever wonder what people hearing this one for the first time are thinking?

- Two idioms that convey positive or negative spin are the *"the glass is half empty" or "the glass is half full."* The former expresses pessimism, the latter, optimism. I distinctly remember the first time I heard this from a teacher and thinking to myself, "What on earth did she just say?"

- Having a *"leg up."* The meaning of this is to have an advantage. The literal translation is a bit confusing. Staying with body parts, there is also *"putting your best foot forward"* which is intended to mean doing your best or using your strengths to cause a positive outcome. How many people learning English do you think would arrive at that conclusion?

- Then there is an idiom that is almost exclusively used for men: *"fall guy."* This means a scapegoat (another idiom) or someone who takes the blame for something gone wrong. I have never heard anyone say "fall woman" or even the politically correct "fall person." Some people use "guys" to also refer to females, so what do I know? As long as we are on the topic of gender, how many times have you heard someone say "she took it like a woman?" This one is reserved for the males 99.9 percent of the time.

- I remember the first time I heard the phrase *"a rolling stone gathers no moss."* I was asked to define the meaning of the phrase by a psychologist who was conducting a personality test. I can't recall exactly how I responded, but I know it was not the meaning he was looking for because he gave me a look like he had just eaten a raw onion. Subsequently, I asked several people what they thought it meant and found it interesting that some people had no clue, others made up something just like I had, and very few accurately said it described people without roots or who did not take responsibility for things.

- My daughter absolutely hates it when I say, *"put it in the bank,"* perhaps because I use the phrase often. I say it to mean that something is a sure thing. The meaning was not confusing to her; she just did not like it. Another problem with idioms and catchphrases is that they can be very irritating to some people. Trust me; since my daughter told me how much she loathes hearing "put it in the bank," I'm very conscious not to say it when she is around.

- This next catchphrase I remember hearing for the first time from a community activist. She was trying to get the company I worked for at the time to make a donation to the organization she represented. She also wanted one of our executives to serve on her organization's board of directors. In the course of our discussion, she asked me who the *"movers and shakers"* were in our company. After politely asking her what she meant, she informed me that she was looking for someone who was influential, with a reputation for getting things done.

It would have taken me forever to come up with the correct interpretation of what she was asking, which reinforces my strong belief that there is no such thing as a stupid question!

- *"Walk the talk."* I actually like this one. Regardless, this phrase can still confuse. Its meaning is "to do what you say you are going to do." I'm a strong believer that talk is cheap (yet another idiom). People say things all the time that they don't mean. Accordingly, the concept of "walking the talk" is important and highly valued by co-workers although the phrase itself is potentially confusing.

- *"With all due respect."* This phrase does not require interpretation so much as an understanding of how it is often used. Many people say, "with all due respect" and mean the direct opposite. Usually, "with all due respect" is followed by an all-out attack on the recipient of the feigned respect. Pay close attention the next time you hear someone say it. Often it is delivered without an ounce of sincerity. If someone prefaces a response to you with this phrase, beware. There may be a hammer about to hit you.

- *"I'd like to echo that remark."* As I look back on my career, I can't begin to estimate the amount of time I spent in meetings. As we all know, many meetings are an abysmal waste of time. There are meetings where the subject matter could have been covered on a memo about the size of a piece of confetti. Then there are the meetings that are scheduled for two hours and end up taking the entire day. More often than not, this occurs thanks to a select breed of Dumb Ass, specifically, the ones who find it necessary to comment on almost every single point made at a meeting. For example, when they are not the ones to initially make an important point, their standard line is, "I'd like to echo that remark." What they really mean is, "I'm upset I did not bring that point up first and want to get some credit for it." If that isn't bad enough, "I'd like to echo that remark" is never the end of it. Then they go on to repeat everything that was already said, not adding a single shred of added value to the discussion.

- The last of these everyday-life catchphrases is my favorite. There are actually two variations. One is **"let me be perfectly honest with you."** A variation is **"that is the honest truth."** Again, the translation is clear; it is the use that is troublesome. If you preface anything you say with either of these terms, the implication is that everything else you say is not honest. Most people say this in a harmless manner, while, with others, it makes you wonder.

Sports-related catchphrases or analogies used in business:

- **"Knock it out of the ball park."** The meaning here is that someone did something really good. In baseball, it means hitting a home run, which is a good thing. Forget about people who don't speak English; what about the people who don't know anything about baseball? The same logic applies to the sport phrases that follow.

- Another baseball phrase is **"three strikes and you're out."** It's used to imply that someone has already made a couple of mistakes and one more will have serious consequences. Another catchphrase with a similar meaning is **"you are living on borrowed time."** Somewhat gruesome, don't you think?

- Since I'm not an avid golfer, the first time I heard this next one, I was truly confused. *"Just grip it and rip it"* translates as "clear your mind and swing at the ball." It can be used as an instruction to stop over-thinking something. I was even more confused to hear *"it's time to let the big dog eat."* This term is used in a number of sports scenarios. Among golfers, it means it's time to use the driver when, previously, the player has only been using his irons. I can just imagine the non-golfers reading this asking what in the world I'm talking about. Well, imagine when I heard this phrase in a work setting to mean that it was time for a person to use new skills to improve his performance. It did not help that this line came from an individual who was incapable of uttering three sentences without injecting some sports analogy. A good friend told me that at the University of Georgia, whose mascot is a bulldog, the phrase "let the big dog eat" is often used at sporting events and means the players from Georgia are ready to beat their opponents. This makes more sense to me than using the phrase in golf or business, but what do I know?

- And finally, for the outdoors sportsmen and women, here are two of my favorite catchphrases that have no business being said in the workplace. The first is *"like shooting fish in a barrel."* Are there really nuts out there who do this? Think about the literal translation of this phrase! The meaning is that something will be easy to do or require minimal effort. Less traumatic, but equally baffling, is *"that dog won't hunt,"* which means whatever you are proposing or recommending will not work.

Idioms and catchphrases primarily used in business settings:

- *"Creating Buzz."* Usually this is in reference to creating excitement about a product. Some try to stretch its application and use it to try to create excitement about a new strategy or program. I personally don't like anyone buzzing me about anything.

- *"Low-hanging fruit"* is a phrase used, for my taste, way too much. It refers to things that are easy to do or accomplish and is often used in the context of a new project or initiative.

- *"Drop dead date."* This morbid phrase is applied to just about any deadline that can occur in a business, for example projects, product introductions, proposals, etc.

- *"Sweat Equity."* This one gets people checking their arm pits—which is always fun—but it refers to someone who has achieved some measure of financial success via their hard work as opposed to having inherited their wealth or obtained it through other indirect means. A different example of Sweat Equity, is someone who contributes to a new venture not by investing money but by doing work for free.

- *"Human Capital."* This is a relatively new term referring to the people who work in an organization. As a Human Resources professional, I particularly dislike this one. As if some organizations aren't sufficiently inhuman, let's now compound the issue by referring to people as if they are a line item on a balance sheet. Another somewhat demeaning analogy is the *"Food Chain,"* at least when it is applied to the hierarchy of an organization. When used in a business context, the term implies that the higher you are in the food chain, the more important you are. People who believe they are important only if they are high in the food chain certainly don't want to be among the bottom feeders (another idiomatic phrase).

- *"Hatchet man"* is another phrase that tends to be heard only in the male context. In business it is often used to describe the person in an organization who is assigned unpleasant, distasteful or ruthless tasks (think mass firings or layoffs). Why is it, however, that you hardly ever hear the term "hatchet woman?"

- How many times have you been at a meeting and someone is asked to provide input and perspective about another person? If the perspectives start with *"he or she is a nice person... but"* you just know the rest is not going to be good. I have often wondered what causes people to inject something good about a person before they go on to rip them, or their work product, to shreds.

- *"Organic growth"* is intended to mean the growth or expansion of an enterprise through internal, rather than external, resources. An external source might be buying a product or a business from another enterprise. Some also refer to it as the financing of the business from internal, rather than external, sources. External, in this case, may mean borrowing. As if business terms weren't difficult enough, do we really need "organic" anything?

Below is a list of phrases that probably originated with a consultant and are now commonly used in the corporate arena:

- *"The elephant in the room."* This is a euphemism used to describe something of high importance that people are afraid or hesitant to acknowledge due to perceived or actual negative consequences. Alternates are the "moose," the "duck" or the "gorilla" in the room.

- *"The body of work."* Usually, this term is used in reference to some project where a lot of work was involved, but only a fraction of it is now evident or getting any attention. Unfortunately, a lot of people who use this term probably created a lot of unnecessary work to begin with and now want credit for it.

- *"Take the pulse of the business."* This is intended to mean getting input on what is really happening in the business or getting input on something that you want to do. In my opinion, it is a rather unfortunate term. Most people have their pulse taken only when they are dying or sick; neither case is good. If you don't know what is going on in your business, taking the pulse won't get you there.

- *"Robust proposal."* This means that a proposal that has been thoroughly researched and the related recommendations are strong. This is a crock of manure because, until you take something to market or implement a new process or program, you won't know if it will work. "Robust" is often Barbarian Speak for "we did all the work we needed to do to cover our behinds if something goes wrong." A related term is *"comprehensive approach or solution."* What this usually means is that you are trying to be all things to all people, which means, in many cases, that you end up disappointing everybody.

- How many times have you read an email or a newspaper article announcing the appointment of a person to a prominent position in a company and the term *"uniquely qualified"* is used? I often wonder if they are trying to make the schmucks that didn't get the job feel better or if they are just **"blowing smoke,"** a phrase that means exaggerating or deceiving. I always laugh when one of the uniquely qualified people fails miserably, and the person who wrote the initial announcement then has to explain what happened with this very special person.

Clear and concise communication is essential in a fast-paced environment. Distracting or unclear idiosyncrasies make it difficult, if not at times impossible, to get all parties on the same page. All of us are guilty of using a favorite phrase or idiom, and, at times, over-using it. Challenge yourself to eliminate from your professional communication phrases that may be misunderstood by, if not outright irritating to, others. When someone is unclear because of style or use of verbiage, the only way forward is to politely ask for clarity by asking the person to rephrase or restate their point in plain English and without theatrics and distractions.

The Use of Spin

Politicians are famous for using spin. While most attempts at spin don't involve outright lies, they do involve making things seem different from what they are, leaving just enough room for conflicting interpretations. Two of my all-time favorite, most blatant attempts by politicians to spin the truth came from former presidents Richard Nixon and Bill Clinton. These two examples were attempts at spin that turned out to be outright lies.

Nixon's most infamous attempt to spin concerned the break-in at the National Democratic Committee's headquarters in Washington DC's Watergate Complex. Commenting on the break-in, Nixon tried to spin it by saying, "I can say categorically that... no one in the White House staff, no one in this Administration, presently employed, was involved in this very bizarre incident." The whole cover-up unraveled, and several people were indicted and convicted, including members of the president's staff. The incident also resulted in Nixon's ignominious resignation from office.[1]

Clinton stood before the TV cameras and said to the country, "I did not have sexual relations with that woman, Miss Lewinsky. I never told anybody to lie, not a single time; never. These allegations are false, and I need to go back to work for the American people." I wonder what was going through Clinton's mind when he made that statement. As the highest-ranking official in our country and arguably the most powerful person on the planet, did he think the incident with Lewinsky was just a harmless dalliance and no one else's business? Or, as with Nixon, did he really believe that spinning was the convenient approach?[2, 3]

A term that you may have heard used in reference to politics over the past few years is "kicking the can down the road." The term refers to the reality that our politicians don't have the will to make the necessary budget cuts today, so they avoid it by "kicking the can down the road" for someone else to deal with it in the future. The restructuring of Medicare and Social Security to make them viable for future recipients are examples of this mentality. Why not call it what it really is: irresponsible.

Did you ever wonder if any politician thinks he ever lost a debate? Does it concern you, as it does me, that after each debate, reporters go to what is literally known as a "Spin Room," where they can hear from each candidate's staff about how their candidate won the debate? First of all, I could care less who won or lost; I'm more interested in what was, or was not, said. Did the candidates show conviction or evasiveness? Did they sound like they knew what they were talking about, or did they just repeat prepared talking points? I don't need some talking puppet telling me what my opinion should be. Before I die, I'd like to see a politician who fared poorly in a debate or misfired on a speech go before the cameras, for the whole world to see, and say, "You know what? I sucked, and I don't deserve your vote."

Finally, in the last few years, the term "leading from behind" has been used to describe our country's position regarding international affairs, including the use of military force in foreign countries. "Leading from behind" isn't spinning; it is an oxymoron. You either lead, or you don't. If you choose not to lead, then you are following. As a follower, you are, at best, providing recommendations that someone else decides whether to adopt or dismiss. At the end of the day, someone has to make the decisions.

Moving to the corporate world, the Barbarians try to spin on a regular basis. They do it to avoid discomfort or conflict. Some do it in attempts to soften bad news. Regrettably, some do it with a clear intent to deceive. Whatever their intentions, more often than not, the spin is not effective. In the first place, employees with even half a brain will see through the attempt. Also, the greater the spin, the more inevitable it is that it will collide head-on with reality. Here are some examples of corporate speak intended to put a spin on reality:

- **Corporate restructuring.** This usually means layoffs. The more top management in a company makes reference to a pending restructure, the bigger the layoffs.

- **Headwinds.** First of all, headwind is a weather term of primary importance to people who fly planes or sail boats. In the corporate arena, the term is used to soften or deflect what is really going on related to rising costs, adverse legislation, declining markets, etc.

- I always chuckled at the terse company-wide emails about some person in a high position leaving the company to **"pursue other interests."** The email usually goes on to thank the person for all her years of service. What all that translates to, in most cases, is that the person got fired.

I once visited a company that enforced a policy of not firing people at certain executive levels for performance problems. Instead, they would communicate that the person had been reassigned to a special project, and they would transfer the person to an office, usually located offsite, until the person secured another job or decided to retire. When the person eventually left, another message would be sent explaining that the person was no longer with the company.

- Some executives will offer trite, if not outright illogical, answers to tough questions about significant challenges to the business. Their superficial answers are mostly born of ignorance or because they simply can't give good answers. That they don't admit that and ask for help has always baffled me. No logical person expects anyone to know all the answers.

- Then there are the top leaders who try to bury bad news. Be it sales declines or other major issues adversely impacting the business, some leaders believe that, by sticking their heads in the sand, employees will, too, and that the adverse conditions will disappear. Doing this in a publicly traded company is foolhardy at best. In a privately held company, you can probably hide reality longer, but it eventually catches up. No matter how much people try to spin the truth, it does not change it. Eventually, the truth will come out. When it does, if employees and other stakeholders feel like they have been deceived, the reactions and consequences are often harsher than if the truth had been told initially.

When tough times hit a company, there is one Golden Rule which must be followed, and that is to ensure that leadership clearly communicates how the situation will impact employees. Leadership has to answer the question of how the situation will affect all employees. If they don't, employees will create their own reality, which oftentimes leads to worry and uncertainty, neither of which is healthy or productive for the organization.

> *"Straight talk is always better than spinning messages. Great leaders create 'followership.' People WANT to work for great leaders. People want to do whatever is possible to deliver great results for leaders they respect and trust. Leaders who are authentic create followership more quickly and at a*

deeper level than those who are not authentic. Leaders who 'spin' messages do not create followership. No matter how crafty they believe they are, the spin is always transparent. Unfortunately, as a result, every message they convey is then perceived as 'spin' (even when that it is not the case). Once a leader starts spinning, all trust is lost."

— STEVE RUSSELL, SENIOR VICE PRESIDENT, HUMAN RESOURCES, McDONALD'S CORPORATION

The Downside of "PC"

I strongly believe that an excess of political correctness (PC) stifles candid discussion in many corporate environments. There was clearly a time when insensitive and crude oratory was out of control. Unfortunately, the pendulum has now swung so far in the other direction that some people are afraid to offer opinions or ask what they may perceive as a potentially insensitive question, in many forums. It seems that, every time I turn on the news, there is someone expressing how offended they are about what someone else said. What I find interesting is that they then go on to vilify the guilty party for their gross indiscretion. "Offended" is now the key word-of-the-day for anything you don't agree with.

People will say wrong things. Sometimes it's done out of sheer stupidity or malice, but, more often than not, it is because of benign ignorance. People make mistakes. Most people don't know about the nuances of every culture, much less an individual's preferences. If every time someone makes a mistake, they get jumped on and publicly vilified, then the next victim will be open and candid discourse. When that happens, decision making will suffer.

Please, don't think for a second that I believe that there are no more crass and bigoted people. There certainly are, and, when they are exposed, they should be dealt with decisively but privately. At the same time, we need to allow people the freedom to make mistakes, even when some of the errors are not politically correct. When the mistakes do occur, they should be addressed with the intent to educate rather than castigate.

Just as Barbarian behaviors can result in frustration for coworkers and add to the complexity of organizations, confusing, misleading or suppressed communications can result in the same. Accordingly, I believe it is important to underscore a belief to which I have always subscribed: To be effective and respected, you should say what you mean and mean what you say. As such, I encourage you to speak with conviction and respect in a straightforward manner and in plain English.

CHAPTER EIGHT

When Organizations Grow Too Fast

I have worked for relatively small companies, big companies, companies that were retracting and companies that were growing. For me, the growing companies were the most fun, but I learned that growth does not come without some pain, including the risk of an increase in the number of Barbarians. Because it affects people in corporations in many ways, growth makes the need for Warriors more critical and the existence of Barbarians more frustrating.

The name of the game in the free capitalist system is to make money and more money. To generate more cash, you have to increase revenue, be more efficient or better yet, do both. Especially if you are a publicly held company, you must use a plan to achieve profitable growth because that is what excites the shareholders and potential investors. Growth, however, is easier said than done. Untapped markets or the opportunity to steal market share from competitors is all well and good, but optimizing opportunities doesn't happen by osmosis.

As companies grow, so does complexity. Depending on the industry, growth may result in more government oversight. Growth requires the need for capital and varying sources from which to obtain it. Growth also usually requires bigger space or more locations and usually extra people. Since this book is about people, let's focus on how growth can impact the people in an organization. Below are a few examples:

- Almost all departments within the enterprise grow with the company. As departments expand, there is a corresponding need to hire and/or train more people. That can result in an increase in the number of subject matter experts who may know the function but not the paying customer. This is always a dangerous situation.

  As departments grow, there is also a higher probability that incompetent, if not outright Dumb Ass, employees will find space to hide.

  As more people are hired, the chances of making bad hires increase. So, too, does the risk of promoting the wrong people (Barbarians) into leadership roles. Some people are promoted out of loyalty or because they were very good at a certain technical expertise. Both are insufficient reasons for promoting a person into a leadership role. The skills required by a leader, especially in a growing enterprise, are not born out of loyalty or subject matter expertise. Effective leaders require a separate set of traits.

  Poor leadership can cause a growing company to be a breeding ground for Barbarians. The incidence of cronyism can increase as leaders seek comfort during periods of high growth. If the leaders are in the Barbarian category, they will most likely bring into the organization cronies who are also Barbarians.

It is also possible during times of growth that change in leadership will occur at the very top of the organization. As an example, it is not uncommon for the founder of a company to be encouraged to leave or be fired. I have always found it interesting when the founder is shown the door. One reason this happens is that the skills it takes to create a breakthrough product or service are not necessarily the skills necessary to lead a growing and increasingly complex company. To be fair, the person's inability to lead a more complex organization is not always the reason for their departure; sometimes founders are ousted because of political infighting or other reasons that have nothing to do with their leadership ability. A case in point is the late, great Apple founder Steve Jobs, who was shown the door only to return a few years later to lead the company to unprecedented success.[1]

Avoiding most of the above maladies requires discipline and a strategy. It takes discipline to hire and promote the right people. A plan and thoughtful execution are required to ensure that, as the company grows, there are successors in place to replace people in key positions (especially leadership positions). When in doubt, I'm an advocate of taking longer to fill a key job than succumbing to what is often self-imposed pressure to get the position filled. For entry- and mid-level hires, establishing a probationary period is worth consideration. It is prudent to ensure that the people you hire are not simply competent but also complement the culture. At any level, for any position, it is a much less painful and damaging course to admit a mistake has been made and make a change. In the case of a leader or mid-level person who is not working out, demotion or transfer may be practical alternatives to separation from the company. At the entry level, if the person does not complement the culture, separation is usually the best alternative. If the issue is poor performance, the entry-level person may have been misplaced, and considering another role should be considered.

As the number of people in the organization increases, so does the need for better and different communication. The need to keep people informed about important things impacting the business becomes paramount. There is also the need to ensure clear and timely intra- and inter-departmental communication.

It is inevitable that, as growth occurs, there is a higher likelihood of miscommunication on important issues. Sometimes communications are not conveyed on a timely basis to the people who need it. More common is the incidence of messages being misinterpreted as they are disseminated throughout the organization.

Another important form of communication that can be adversely impacted by growth is idea sharing. Ideas can impact the business in a myriad of ways, including how to do things more efficiently, product innovation, better ways of servicing the customer, cost-saving recommendations, etc.

To ensure that the quality of communications is maintained at a reasonably high level and to continue to encourage the generation of ideas, I believe leadership needs to think small. What I mean is that leadership needs to find or create communication forums that get them close to employees and make it comfortable for employees to ask for and share important information. Emails are sometimes unavoidable, for example, where there is quick-breaking news or urgent information to be disseminated. To rely solely on email, however, is too impersonal and risky. It's dicey because some messages may be misinterpreted or ignored. Two-way interactive communications is best, for example, a town hall-type meeting where leadership meets face-to-face with employees. Whenever practical, meetings between leaders and employees, on employee turf and involving face-to-face discussions about the business, are invaluable. Conference calls that employees can join to interact with top management are not as ideal as a face-to-face forum, but they are sometimes the most practical. Although I'm not a big fan of videos, sometimes they make sense to ensure leadership is reaching a wide audience and that everyone is hearing the same, unfiltered, message.

- Growth tends to create bureaucracy. Bureaucracy can mean more layers of approval for certain expenditures, additional policies or procedures and extra people involved in making decisions. One side effect of bureaucracy is the need for more things being put in writing, including the use of manuals that can range from product information to how people should conduct themselves at work. At some level, these attempts to capture things in writing are good in that they strive for consistency. But they cross the line when the manual or policy craze begins to overburden employees and, by extension, the overall business.

My preference is this: the less documentation a company needs to successfully operate, the better. Moreover, I believe a culture that challenges bureaucracy is a good thing. Otherwise, a company can quickly find itself choking on manuals, cumbersome processes and inefficient layers of approval and oversight. To create and sustain a culture that challenges unnecessary bureaucracy requires controlled and practical leadership. Specifically, it requires the discipline to regularly challenge bureaucracy and the common sense to know where and how much is necessary. Left to the Barbarians, bureaucracy will reign. There are armies of consultants who earn a living helping companies eliminate bureaucracy, including simplifying, if not totally getting rid of, processes.

I worked in two companies where some of the employees were represented by unions. In both cases, it was my primary responsibility to represent the company in dealing with union issues, including contract negotiation and grievance resolution. It is no secret that, when a union represents employees, the amount of documentation about work rules can reach nauseating levels. Also, the amount of documentation necessary to address issues can be cumbersome. In some cases, dealing with union issues becomes more about endurance than what is good for either the employees or the business. Some companies, in their attempts to stay union-free, invent work rules that can be so cumbersome and inefficient that they might as well have a union.

As the business grows, leadership should challenge existing and new processes to ensure they are adding value rather than detracting from it. Some processes, unfortunately, have nothing to do with value. Instead, they focus on fiduciary responsibilities. These processes should be sufficiently strong to satisfy the fiduciary need but not exceed what is prudent.

- As most companies grow, so do the layers of management. There are companies with a board of directors, a president and/ or chief executive officer, a chief operating officer, executive vice presidents, senior vice presidents, assistant vice presidents, senior directors, directors, senior managers and on and on, all the way down to the entry-level workers. The more layers there are, the harder it is to do anything. If Barbarians in key positions exacerbate the growing number of layers, it can make getting things done agonizing.

Some management experts believe that six to 10 direct reports is ideal; others argue that as many as 25 is manageable with today's technology. Some say it depends, which is where I weigh in. Keeping track of employee results, training and communicating are much improved from even ten years ago. While technology is potentially capable of bringing people closer together, it also has the disadvantage of allowing the Barbarians to avoid their managers. Some people require more oversight than others. Achieving a proper balance starts, I believe, with a focus on keeping the organization as flat as possible and maintaining the conviction to challenge attempts to increase the number of layers of management. More importantly, a strong understanding of your organization's available talent is invaluable. Where possible, look for opportunities to build and, at the appropriate time, disband self-directed teams. It is also prudent to challenge all leaders to encourage employee autonomy, but, to do so successfully, you need Warriors. To give Barbarians too much autonomy is like inviting Rasputin to be part of the family.

Finally, ensure that the layers of leadership that are in place communicate often and get together as much as is practical to discuss the business and share best practices. Above all, top leadership must be maniacal about ensuring people at all levels understand the difference between management and leadership.

"Managing is not leading. The two should not be confused. Conversely, you don't have to have a big title to be and to

act like a leader. We easily transpose the words 'leader-ship' and 'management' to describe those people who are at the top of an organization. After decades of working for and observing the characteristics of people running organizations, it is evident that there are an abundance of managers and a dearth of real leaders. Furthermore, it is more likely that a great 'leader' will also possess and exhibit sound management skills, but few of those people I would describe as 'manager' also have great leadership skills. I don't minimize the importance of great managers. Their role is essential to success. However, I distinguish that skill set from great leaders who can move an organization past the boundaries that it may have created for itself and have extraordinary success. Oftentimes, unfortunately, some managers will be the prime reason why boundaries exist in the first place."

— MIKE ANDRES, CHAIRMAN AND CHIEF EXECUTIVE
OFFICER, LOGAN'S ROADHOUSE INC.

- The most difficult thing for a company to sustain is its culture. Culture is also the most important attribute of a growing enterprise. That is, of course, if it is a healthy and productive culture. In most cases, it is difficult to achieve sustained and profitable growth without a healthy culture. When I refer to culture, I believe it includes not only how the employees interact and cooperatively work and learn from each other, but more importantly, how they interact and treat the paying customer. Companies may become successful because of a breakthrough product or service, but true success occurs when those product or service ideas are combined with a creative, efficient and fun culture. I'm referring to the kind of culture where employees are energized and look forward to coming to work and leadership engenders and rewards Warrior behaviors.

They are employees who are committed to doing things the right way and to the success of the enterprise.

The culture of a company, when it gets it right, is the most difficult thing for the competition to replicate. Competitors can relatively easily steal product and service ideas from other companies. Why is culture so hard to replicate? Because leaders are the people who primarily shape and nurture it. Leaders who try to emulate a healthy culture from another company can understand intellectually what makes it so. They can also articulate the elements of that healthy culture. But if their actions and behaviors don't nourish it, all the intellectualizing in the world won't make it happen.

Staying close to the customer is one way to ensure that the leadership of the enterprise won't get to a point where it is talking only to itself. On the employee side of the equation, the communication and reinforcement of the company's values are essential to maintaining the culture. The concept of storytelling can be effective in reinforcing the culture as the company grows. In particular, storytelling about the treatment of customers and events that define what makes the company a special enterprise works.

Early in my career, I had a colleague at the executive level whose career began in a very large organization. Over the years he had, by design, sought opportunities in smaller and smaller companies. Once I asked him why he did so, as I assumed that, financially, he was making less and less as he moved from one company to another. His answer was as follows: Firstly, he said he had made enough money so environment was much more appealing than compensation. Regarding compensation, he posed the question, "How much money is enough?" He said many people chase money at the expense of family and health, and to him it was not that important. Finally, he said he had too many experiences in which growth had created more complexity but not more profits. "Juan," he said, "you'd be amazed at the number of companies that make a 10% profit on $100 million in sales and then end up making 5% on $200 million in sales and wonder what went wrong."

Especially for publicly traded companies, profitable growth is imperative. Accordingly, before a company declares that it will double or triple in size, it is wise to have thoroughly done its homework about what that means, especially from a people perspective. Moreover, it is important to understand not only what impact the company's growth will have on the existing people but also to have a plan for how to recruit, train and acculturate new people.

CHAPTER NINE

Things I Learned Along
the Way

In the introduction, I mentioned that I was a part of Corporate America for over 37 years. Prior to my professional experience, I held several part-time and summer jobs, beginning at the age of 14 until I graduated from undergraduate school. These jobs included, among others, being a laborer on a cement construction crew, a janitor, a dishwasher and a restaurant manager. As such, my views about people in organizations have been shaped both by my professional experience as well as my prior years working in a wide variety of jobs.

In this chapter, I will cover some things that I believe deserve reinforcing as well as share significant things I learned in my journey. All of these things I learned from Warriors and Barbarians. All were great lessons for me.

- *Important things that impact the business need to be aired and discussed, regardless of how unpleasant or painful they may be.* Where possible, unpleasant things must be brought to closure, or at the very least, their impact on the organization should be understood so it can be managed.

A Barbarian's inclination is to suppress unpopular or unpleasant information. To do so is, in essence, to avoid reality. As an example, Barbarians may actively discourage discussion about the success of a competitor or demean its importance. Barbarians may also suppress critical discussion about people they are close to or admire. They make certain issues taboo, refusing to discuss, let alone address, them in a proactive manner. Warriors realize that to forbid surfacing painful issues or to suppress discussion about important issues is not in the organization's best interests.

To forbid or ignore something does not eliminate its existence, much less prevent its adverse impact on the business. Competitors do things that can significantly set back your business. There are people the boss may like who are incompetent and create efficiency and morale issues. If not allowed a proper forum, important issues like these will be hashed and re-hashed anyway. The problem, though, is that they are discussed in forums that, having no official support or guidance, can become breeding grounds for distortion and dissent.

Barbarians suppress unpopular information and eventually pay the price. Warriors create forums where important issues can be proactively discussed and addressed regardless of how unsavory they might be.

• **Rationalizing failure is failure.** Rationalizing failure is the "fool's gold" of the narrow-minded and the egomaniacal. When failure occurs through a person's career, he or she should learn from it, understand it and move on with the resolve not to let it happen again. If history teaches us anything, it is that many people refuse to learn from failure or adversity. As such, they are destined to repeat the failures of those who preceded them. Learning from failure is not just about what you personally experience, it is also about learning from others, about what, and what not, to do.

It has been said that the definition of insanity is doing the same thing over and over again and expecting different results. The Barbarians subscribe to doing the same dumb things over and over and deluding themselves into believing that they will see different results. Warriors learn from failure and adversity and resolve not to repeat the actions and behaviors that caused the failure.

- ***What happens to you in business and in your career is very personal.*** In the context of the corporate world, it is very personal when you don't get the promotion, you receive a bad performance review, your work is considered unacceptable or you get laid off or fired. Don't let anyone one try to convince you otherwise; these things are very personal, primarily because they potentially impact your reputation and even your livelihood. Much worse are situations like Enron, where people lost jobs and retirement savings. Worst of all is the situation where people lose their lives. For the victims and their survivors, it does not get any more personal than that.

Work-life adversity should be taken personally but also channeled toward a positive outcome. I strongly suggest that you learn from adversity and resolve not to let it happen again.

Warriors don't play the victim role. When something bad happens, they take it personally and ensure they take the necessary actions to avoid similar outcomes in the future.

- Being liked is not necessarily a benefit in the corporate world. That is not to suggest that people conduct themselves in a boorish manner. Rather it is, to be very clear, that ***being respected is much more important than being liked.*** Being liked and respected is ideal. The two are not mutually exclusive.

  Some people spend inordinate amounts of time doing things that they perceive will make them popular with co-workers. It is interesting how these people appear shocked when co-workers or the boss tell them to focus on doing the job. Some are incapable of understanding that nice without substance does not cut it.

  Bosses who focus on doing things to be liked by their colleagues and subordinates, rather than doing things to be effective, invariably create aggravation for the very people they are trying so hard to please. When the work fails to get done, there are consequences. Liking the boss at the expense of productivity is not a sustainable situation. Bosses who seek to be popular often avoid making the tough, or what they perceive might be unpopular, decisions. Avoiding decisions or looking for universally popular decisions is pure folly.

  Conversely, respect is a solid foundation on which to position effectiveness and leadership. Co-workers who are perceived as reliable, along with bosses who make thoughtful decisions and accept responsibility are respected. Not all bad bosses are Barbarians. Some bosses are very good people who simply have no business being in a leadership role.

- When we think of large organizations, we seldom think about the people who are part of those organizations. Other than the organization that we work for, most of us know other companies mostly by their products and not by their people. There are some iconic leaders whose names are as familiar to us as their products. The late Steve Jobs is indelibly linked with Apple; so, too, is Bill Gates with Microsoft. But these are the exceptions. When most people think about iconic brands, they don't think about people so much as think about the product. Ninety-nine percent of the population would be hard-pressed to come up with a name of anyone who works for a major brand unless they worked there, too, or knew someone who did. Yet, at Apple and Microsoft, as is in every successful organization, legions of committed people make the great products.

Conversely, when we think about our local merchants, we are much more likely to associate the business with the people. For example, most of us live relatively close to fine-dining restaurants. Our selection of where we eat usually starts with what kind of food we prefer, but once that choice is made, most of us will select a restaurant where the employees create a special atmosphere for the customer. And if you visit the restaurant regularly, you will know at least some of the people by name.

When leadership forgets that it is people who make a brand, they also forget that people can also sink a brand. If leadership diminishes the importance of people and begins to treat them like commodities, the brand will eventually wither on the vine of apathy. *People make the brand, not the other way around.*

- I once heard someone say that if you honor your children, they will honor you. I thought that was an excellent concept and one that great leaders practice with their subordinates. In the workplace, *leaders who treat people with dignity and respect and take an interest in their growth and success will benefit from their loyalty.*

Sometimes honoring your employees requires courage, but the loyalty and respect you get in return is inestimable.

"I grew up with old-fashioned values and a family who demonstrated a very strong work ethic. My father used to tell us that he didn't care if we swept streets for a living, but we better give it 100%. It was no surprise that I embraced those values and took them to work with me every day.

"These values served me well in my career ... I had regular promotions and excellent performance reviews, but something was holding me back ... I realize now that the only thing holding me back was me. I came to that realization because of two tremendous leaders I encountered on my career journey. They changed my life.

"I spent most of my career working in the Midwest area of the country, where a conservative mindset was valued and embraced. I thrived in many aspects of my work, but I always left a big part of me at home ... my life with my same-sex partner was never discussed at work.

"I was ready to move forward in my career but couldn't explain my inability to relocate due to my partner's work. Everyone must have known, but I could never say it. My partner expressed a willingness to take a risk and relocate to a different part of the country, so I applied for a promotion that required relocation but still kept silent about my sexual orientation. I got the job.

"The first of the two impactful leaders entered the situation at this juncture. This leader found out about my home

life and worked behind the scenes to ensure that I received full relocation benefits to be able to move my partner. He reached out to me to tell me what he had done, and I was flabbergasted that anyone would have shared with him such a personal thing about me. This 'nudge' was the first time in my 25-year career that the door was opened for me to bring my full self to work. He has been my strongest and most loyal advocate over the years, and today he constantly serves as a role model in fighting for diversity and equal benefits for gay and lesbian employees.

"The second impactful leader was a man who demonstrated courageous leadership at a time that it wasn't popular to embrace gay and lesbian employees. He was a pioneer in organizing an employee business network for gay and lesbian employees. He did so even though he was not gay. While conservative community groups were picketing our company's sites, he was pioneering the first career symposium for gay and lesbian employees. He stayed true to his beliefs, he stayed strong in the face of adversity, and he gained the respect and admiration of many.

"Today, I still stumble at times when people joke about gays and lesbians or when discriminatory opinions are expressed. I'm still growing in regards to becoming comfortable in my own skin at work. But these two leaders opened the door for me to bring my full self to work for the first time in my life, and I will never, ever go back to that place. I can only hope that I can role model that behavior and have the same impact on others through my own courageous leadership."

— TONI PORODA, FINANCE DIRECTOR,
McDONALD'S CORPORATION

- One of my favorite quotes, and I believe one of the most profound, comes from the French philosopher Voltaire, who said that, ***"Every man is guilty of all the good he did not do."***[1] Doing well for colleagues and subordinates is often rewarded but always rewarding.

My daughter is a charge nurse in a labor and delivery unit in an inner-city hospital where most of the patients are indigent. The stories she has told me about her experiences with patients range from the tragic to the heart-warming. The thing, however, that has stuck with me the most is when she said, "Dad, I really believe that random acts of kindness can literally change lives."

Specifically, she told me that she would do things for patients or family, not thinking anything of it, and then be rewarded with unexpected appreciation from the people she touched. I'm also blessed with a spouse who has a reputation for giving of herself to anyone in need. She will go out of her way to help family, friends, neighbors and even strangers however and whenever she can. It is amazing how much people appreciate her (and probably can't fathom why she married a slug like me).

Don't be guilty of all the good you didn't do. Look for ways to help people every day, and you will be richer for it. I truly believe that the more you help others to succeed, the more you will succeed.

- Have you ever heard the jazz ditty "Tain't What You Do It's the Way That You Do It?" Though it's a fun song, the message is wrong: ***It is both what, and how, you do it that matters.*** How you do things is important and differentiates the great from the good. The primary premise of this book is about how you do things will define who you are and if you are at the Warrior or Barbarian end of the spectrum. That said, what you do is also critical. If you are focusing on ineffective things, the greatest style in the world won't get you too far. If your products and services are not appealing to the customer, style alone won't get you very far. It is both what you do and the way that you do it.

- Ability and will are two very different things. Many people have the ability to be leaders, but ability without the will won't get it done. By having the will to lead, I specifically mean things like:

  o Inspiring others
  o Having moral courage to do what is right rather than what may be comfortable or expedient
  o Making the hard, sometimes gut-wrenching, decisions
  o Accepting that detractors will second-guess you
  o Accepting criticism
  o Being willing to take risks and to fail

There are people throughout organizations who are not in positions of authority but are proven leaders. There are people with fancy titles who are horrible leaders. *Warrior Leaders possess the will to lead.* They accept the responsibilities that come with being at the helm.

- *Capitalism does not reward effort. It rewards results.* Moreover, it rewards consistent results over time. You can't go in front of shareholders and say, "We tried really hard, but we just didn't make any money" or "We know the product is great; we just can't convince the customers of that." That is not to say that people don't become enamored with a company or even an industry and pay ridiculous amounts of money for the stock of unproven companies. The boom in the stock of technology companies, and its subsequent bust often referred to as the Dotcom Bubble of the late 1990s, is an example. Some of the so-called Dotcom companies failed, and some were sold at a fraction of their peak stock price.[2] Whether it's a company's efforts that do not lead to results or stockholder hubris, the outcome is the same: Companies that don't produce results will eventually fail or be sold to someone who can make them work.

All companies require results and, in turn, demand the same from their employees. Companies where the drive for results is relentless and unforgiving are not for the meek of heart. You may have heard the phrase, "What does not kill you makes you stronger." I have worked for companies that tried to kill me every day. People who are not results-oriented will not do well in companies that are relentless about results. In these companies, people who are not results-oriented either give up and quit or are most likely asked to leave. Those who stick it out do so with an understanding of what it takes to thrive and the resolve to consistently deliver results.

- Unless a position requires special degrees or certifications, ***don't dismiss the value of street smarts.*** People with degrees deserve credit for their commitment to improve themselves. However, you should not dismiss an individual simply because she doesn't hold a post-high school degree. Books may help with the intangibles of how to interact with others, along with management and leadership, but words and theory have to be converted into meaningful actions and behaviors. Part of intuition involves common sense and the ability to read people and situations and take the appropriate actions. Street-smart people possess that ability. While not a universal truth, street-smart people usually tap into life experiences that helped them develop a keen sense of people and situations.

Being book-smart may also help in the understanding of concepts and abstract thoughts. We often attribute high intelligence to those who are well-educated and well-read, but if the person doesn't possess a lick of common sense, he will struggle in situations where regular interaction with others is important. Moreover, street-smart people are not incapable of learning concepts or abstract thoughts. Some of the most intelligent people I know who had the ability to grasp complexity relatively easily had very little formal education. There are jobs that don't require significant amounts of interaction that a book-smart person with limited social skills can do well.

However, for jobs requiring intelligence and the ability to be effective in dynamic situations, don't dismiss the value of street-smart individuals. Finally, street-smart people can spot bullshit a mile away. They are especially adept at identifying and managing the Egomaniacs.

- *Try not to worry about situations and events that you cannot control.* Worrying about things you can't control only adds stress to your work and home life. If there are things you can't control with potential, adverse material impact on you, the best thing I have learned is to create acceptable alternatives for yourself. For example: You find yourself in a situation where pending layoffs could cost you your job. You can either make yourself invaluable to the company through your leadership and by delivering results, or you can start looking for another job in case the hammer falls. In union environments, contracts and seniority usually dictate who gets laid off first. Because unions are not that prevalent anymore, in most companies, seniority is usually taken into account when making layoff decisions. Still, most companies will do what they can to keep the most talented and productive employees.

Other situations beyond your control may include the company being sold, the elimination of products or services, etc. Regardless of what it is don't fret; instead, act to ensure the best outcome for yourself.

If you are ever in a situation where leaving the company is the best alternative, as much as is practical, try and go to something better. People can get restless to find a new job when they find themselves in the types of situations mentioned. Most people also get antsy to move when they have an insufferable boss or are surrounded by a collection of Barbarian co-workers. Regardless of the motive to find another job, you should treat it as an opportunity to improve your situation rather than going for the sake of leaving and potentially finding yourself in a worse situation. Departing for something better requires homework about the new opportunity and thoughtful consideration of all the pros and cons.

- *Evaluate and deal with people objectively to avoid being blindsided by their frailties.* In the workplace, try not to get too high on people you like or even consider friends. If you do and they fail to deliver or disappoint you, in some ways that can be much worse than being let down by the people you think of as Barbarians.

One of the most common ways that people will disappoint you is by saying things they don't really mean under the guise of being "nice" or "well-meaning." I have never understood this mentality. If you say something you don't believe, it can turn into disappointment for the person to whom you said it. Your words may lead someone to believe that you care about them or about their work or that you will be supportive, when, in reality, you have no intention of doing either.

Worse than the shallow or insincere pronouncements are the commitments that people don't keep. Some people make commitments to support you in some way, but when it comes time for them to follow through, they don't. There can be many reasons for the lack of follow-through: Circumstances can change that make it difficult for the person to keep his commitment; the person was just being "nice" and never intended to follow through; or the person does not have the ability or the resources to follow through. People who commit to doing things without the conviction to follow through could learn from Ben Franklin, who said, "Well done is better than well said."[3]

Regardless of why someone fails to deliver on his commitment, you are the one who potentially suffers. Accordingly, the more important the issue, the more crucial it is to ensure that you have a Plan B or even C. If at all practical, you should also be wary of relying on one person for essential support. It will serve you well to explore as many options as possible for whatever support you may need.

While it may be hard to accept it when people you like and admire disappoint you, it is bound to happen. Stay ahead of it by being objective about people, what they say and their record with past commitments. More importantly, ensure you have alternatives to address the more important things.

- Staying with the concept of planning and, specifically, how to deal with issues that can be costly or damaging to the brand, ***it is prudent to plan for the worst-case scenario.*** Terminations can be messy and costly affairs. At times, a termination decision is made for the sake of other employees or the business, even though all the information necessary to withstand legal challenges may not meet the standards that the attorneys would prefer. In such cases, there is a monetary risk if lawsuits ensue or, depending on the circumstances, even a risk to the brand. As such, it is prudent to review all possible worst-case scenarios and have plans in place to deal with each one. It may mean losing litigation, experiencing backlash from other employees or customers, bad public relations and/or compromised intellectual property. Thus, if a strategy to deal with all these worst-case scenarios is in place, anything falling short of the worst is manageable. That is not to suggest that a scenario that falls short of the worst possible outcome won't be painful. Rather, it is to say that when you are faced with a very tough decision without the corresponding assurance that all will turn out well, you make the best possible decision you can based on what is right for the employees and the business and prudently prepare to deal with the consequences.

Tough situations can take many other forms, for example, restructuring the company, the introduction, modification or elimination of products or services, the purchase of another company or, worse yet, some type of catastrophic event. It has been said that the best way to manage a crisis is before it occurs. Managing a crisis is about planning ahead and being ready for the worst.

A key ingredient of planning is the generation of potential solutions. Many people are adept at reacting to and managing chaos, but they are not as valuable as those people who are good at preventing it. Furthermore, when chaos occurs or the unexpected happens, it is important not to just solve the problem at hand but also to review the broader implications of why it occurred and ensure it does not happen again. In short, don't just treat the illness. Eliminate it.

Nothing is guaranteed in life or business. Careers are made or lost by how people manage challenging situations. Some credit is given to those who react well under extenuating circumstances, but much more credit is bestowed on those who eliminate the possibility of adversity occurring. By anticipating and planning, you can assure much more control, much less time spent reacting and much more success.

- What is behind you, good or bad, is only meaningful if you learn from it. Regardless of the past, you can only try to influence the present and the future. Too many people invest themselves in "what could have been." Conversely, too many people rest on their laurels and forget what got them to their current state. *It does not matter where you came from; it matters where you are going.*

- *Nothing can substitute for dedication to a goal and an uncompromising passion to succeed.* Too many people accept what they think they deserve instead of going for what they really want. There is an adage in soccer and basketball that you are one 100 percent assured of not scoring if you don't shoot. If you shoot, you might miss, but you at least give yourself the chance of scoring.

People who make a difference don't accept what they get if they have a vision of something different. Here are some examples of people who did not accept what they thought they deserved but rather strived for what they wanted:

- The inventor Thomas Edison spoke for the ages and for all who strive to be better when he said, "I have not failed. I've just found 10,000 ways that won't work." He also said, "Genius is one percent inspiration and 99 percent perspiration."[4]

- Walt Disney initially failed at business, including bankruptcy, before creating an iconic enterprise.[5]

- You may not know Akio Morita, but you have most likely heard of the company he was instrumental in creating: Sony. Expected to take over his family sake and soy sauce business and, at a time when "Made in Japan" was associated with low quality, Morita chose a different route and founded Tokyo Telecommunications Engineering Corp. in a bombed-out department store in the ruins of postwar Tokyo. From an early dream to develop a tape recorder, then a transistor radio, Morita and his partners pushed forward to create a multi-billion dollar company.[6]

Settling for what you get rather than striving for what you want is a defeatist mind-set. If you are a person who enjoys the journey as much as the destination, then striving for what you want is better than accepting the status quo.

- Too much comfort can be perilous. When people get complacent, they start to deteriorate. Important attributes like energy, a sense of urgency and creativity begin to wane. Stress to extremes is unhealthy. On the other hand, comfort and complacency to extremes may not be unhealthy but can certainly be career-threatening.

Some stress can be energizing. If you survive stressful situations, they can make you more resilient. To be sharp and to grow requires some level of discomfort. Certainly trying new approaches to problems or taking risks can be discomforting, but without some level of creativity and risk-taking, you can easily become stale. When people lose their vigor, they lose their edge. Farrah Gray, a successful author, philanthropist and real estate entrepreneur, explains an important reason for his success like this: *"Comfort is the enemy of achievement."*[7, 8]

- How can you deal with an intimidator? First calibrate his or her intentions. Start by asking the perpetrator to repeat whatever he said that caused you to interpret it as an attempt to intimidate you. If your instincts are confirmed, look the perpetrator in the eye (this, by the way, is more important than anything you say, because someone trying to intimidate you doesn't expect that you will stand up to them) and let them know that what they said feels like an attempt to intimidate you and that it is unacceptable. Then tell them exactly what you are going to do about it. This is not easy, by any means, but doing nothing, in most cases, only encourages the intimidator.

At their core, people who try to intimidate others are cowards. They are bullies who, for some perverse reason, get satisfaction from instilling fear or causing humiliation in others. The true sleazebag intimidators are those who are trying to hide something nefarious, and they view you as someone who can expose them. These are the types with whom I had my first experiences. As you might imagine, in Human Resources, you are often asked to investigate situations that can reveal questionable behavior. It can also cause people to act in strange ways. More than once, I was in the midst of investigating some wrongdoing where the bullies came out in force and tried to get me to bury information or to suggest that, if I acted on my findings, there would be dire consequences. These attempts to intimidate me did not work, thankfully, but I have been flabbergasted to see how many people who fall victim to intimidation and consequently do very stupid things.

It is sad but true that there are whistleblower laws to protect employees who report unethical or illegal activity by employers. As hard as it might be, I believe that confronting the issue is always better than falling victim to intimidation. If necessary, seek guidance from mentors or even legal counsel about how to manage the situation, but ***don't let the miscreants get to you.*** If you become weaker, you empower the villains to continue their inexcusable, if not outright illegal, behaviors.

- When you accept a position, you accept the responsibilities that come with it. If you did not do your homework about the situation you were inheriting, there is no one to blame but yourself. Even if you were deceived or misled about the realities of the job, you, unfortunately, still own it. You may not want to stay in the job if the people who hired you misled you, but if you stay, you own it. It is common for people to accept a job only to realize that the challenges were much greater than they appeared to be initially. Or perhaps the work environment is toxic and not what you anticipated. Surprises can occur even if the job is with the same company or you are replacing someone familiar. ***Regardless of the circumstances, when you accept a position and make the decision to stay on the job, you are responsible for it.***

When people hire you into a challenging situation that needs fixing, the expectation is that you will do so. Blaming others for your troubles is abdicating responsibility. If you take the job, you are expected it to do it and everything that comes with it. "I wasn't here when that happened" or "this is worse than I thought it was" are declarations of ineptitude. Warrior Leaders call it as it is and say what they are going to do to fix the situation and get things on the right track. They accept the responsibilities that come with taking on a challenge and move forward with focus on the planning and actions necessary to change the trajectory of the situation for the better.

- *Hope is not a strategy.* The term has been around a long time, and, in my opinion, the sentiment behind the words has been around even longer.

Hope is a desire that something will change for the better or that good or favorable things will happen. Millions and millions also hope that their team will win. Many even bet on it. Sometimes it works, and sometimes it doesn't. Hope can be a powerful emotion. It is a source of strength and, for some, enables them to persevere through adverse situations. Unfortunately for others, hope is all that they may have left. Hope without action, however, is in many cases a temporary respite before an unpleasant reality sets in. If you want to control your destiny, you must take action.

I believe that most of us control much more than we think we do. Taking action when it is possible to shape our lives does not guarantee positive results, but it beats the alternative of doing nothing and relying solely on hope. Reality can be daunting, but when it bites, you need to take the actions necessary to change it.

When it comes to the workplace, hope is not only a lousy strategy, it is also a blueprint for failure. Hoping for a better boss or co-worker, that your recommendations are adopted, that the market will improve and your product sales increase are all precursors to disappointment.

- *Who you spend your time with will greatly influence who you become.* Your work colleagues, friends and family all play a part in shaping your thoughts, perspectives and behaviors. However, only you can decide to what extent they will influence you. I believe that the more time you spend with people who are:

  o Smarter than you, the smarter you will be
  o More articulate than you the, more articulate you will be
  o More assertive than you, the more assertive you will be
  o More enthusiastic than you, the more enthusiastic you will be
  o More thoughtful than you, the more thoughtful you will be

On the other hand, the more time you spend with people with poor attributes or behave poorly, the more those things will shape who you become. Think about the people who had the greatest positive influence in your life. Think also about the people who were the biggest disappointments, and then ask yourself who you'd rather spend time with. People influence who you are and who you become, in subtle ways. Understanding this dynamic can be incredibly helpful in shaping your career.

- *It takes an open mind to understand one's strengths and weaknesses.* Achieving optimum effectiveness requires honest introspection. If you are not introspective, you run a high risk of over-inflating your strengths and underestimating your weaknesses.

In the corporate world, an open mind is also needed to understand your competitors. If you view your competitors with bias and derision, you run the risk of not understanding their strengths and potentially getting beat in the market place. Chinese military man Sun Tzu penned the book *The Art of War* around 500 B.C. Its teachings have been used in warfare, and in business, ever since. This verse from the book simply and profoundly illustrates the importance of introspection:

> *"Therefore I say: Know the enemy and know yourself; in a hundred battles, you will never be in peril. When you are ignorant of the enemy but know yourself, your chances of winning or losing are equal. If ignorant both of your enemy and yourself, you are certain in every battle to be in peril."*[9]

- **Care about what you do. If you don't care, ask yourself why you are doing it, or, better yet, go do something else.** Throughout my career, I have been truly dumbfounded by the myriad of people I encountered who hated what they did but kept on doing it. Maybe it was because they did not know how to do anything else. Perhaps it was a lack of confidence or because they were trapped by circumstances. Whatever the reason, it is most often the case that people who don't like what they are doing are unhappy. Additionally, if you don't appreciate, value and care about the people you work with, the job can be absolute misery.

- ***The higher you ascend in your career and the fancier the titles get, the more time you will spend on "people issues," good or bad.*** Leaders who are uncomfortable about managing the people issues are fooling themselves. Many people are promoted because of technical skills and progress to higher and higher levels, all the while clinging to a desire to focus most of their time on technical, rather than people, issues. The higher you go up the corporate ladder, the importance of developing people in your charge increases. The greater the need to communicate goals and strategies, the need to select the right people for key positions grows. The more important the need to evaluate performance and potential becomes, the need to make the tough decisions to demote or fire people becomes more critical. All of this is not to suggest that there won't be any technical aspects to your work, but it will most surely be less than the time that is required to lead people and manage people issues. Letting go of some of the technical aspects of the job can be difficult, if not impossible, for some. To rely on others for what you once loved to do can be painful. If you find yourself in that position, you should examine whether increasing levels of leadership is the right path for you.

- ***It is advantageous to be flexible when it comes to career decisions.*** At one time or another I have lived in Cuba, Illinois, Florida, Tennessee, Wisconsin and Colorado. As I reflect on my life, there is no way I could have possibly predicted that I would live in all those places. There is also no way I could have foreseen that I would first move to locations where my parents would find work and then places where my career would take me. In almost all the cases, there were concerns about moving away from family and, certainly, moving to unfamiliar environments.

I have known very talented people who bypassed promotional opportunities to stay close to family. To the extent that they were satisfied with their jobs, it was obviously an admirable decision. However, I have also seen people grow frustrated with their positions, specifically, with the lack of upward mobility because of their decision not to relocate. There are no easy answers.

- **Work hard to save up your "go to hell money."** Relatively early in my career, I had the good fortune to rub elbows with a gentleman at the VP level who encouraged me to save money early and often. When I met him, he was in his early fifties, and it was evident that, from a financial perspective, he did not have to work another day in his life. One day I asked him how he had come to be in such a good financial position. He told me that he had started from very humble beginnings and that his dad, who had lived through the Great Depression of the late 1920s and early 1930s, always told him to save money early and often, that money makes more money and that he had to position himself as early as possible to come to work on any given day and be able to say, "Go to hell—I don't need this job anymore. I'm walking away." This is without a doubt one of the most important pieces of advice I have ever received.

My lovely and loving wife, Randi, supported me by bypassing big houses, fancy cars and extravagant vacations until we had enough in the bank to be able to say "go to hell" if it came to that.

I learned a great deal from, and about, people during my career from both the Warriors and the Barbarians. I encourage you to learn from people and from your own experiences, and apply the lessons learned into career-enhancing actions.

CHAPTER TEN

Take Control of your Legacy

I don't believe that people get out of bed every morning and choose to be Barbarians or act in Barbarian ways. I don't believe that people that do dumb things once in a while are inherently Dumb Asses, but when someone does dumb things consistently and it becomes a habit, they join the fraternity or sorority of Dumb Asses. I don't believe that a big ego is necessarily a bad thing, as long as it is kept in its proper place and does not morph into behaviors that hurt others. Many of those who go that route are destined to, sooner or later, crash and burn. I believe that all of us have a choice to be a Warrior or a Barbarian and that most, if not all of us, need help from friends, family, colleagues and mentors to help make our way down the Warrior's path.

I admire capitalism, and more importantly, I cherish and respect our country. The combination of our freedoms and our capitalism, I believe, is the foundation that makes our nation so special and why it attracts people from all over the globe.

In the capitalist arena, companies succeed, and companies fail. Some companies fail even when Warriors are at the helm. There is no shame in failure. The shame comes in not trying. I also believe that, win or lose, capitalism builds character. Finally, I believe it engenders a sense of accountability and responsibility.

My journey through the corporate world has been blessed. I have been privileged to know, work with and develop lasting friendships with some of the best people I could possibly imagine. I was very fortunate in my journey to have worked with many more Warriors than Barbarians. And when I did work with Barbarians, I was fortunate to have a supportive family, colleagues and mentors to help me "stay the course" and keep my sanity. Though my work travels and day-to-day challenges required more time away from family and friends than I would have preferred, I don't regret my decision to pursue a career in the corporate world. While there were sacrifices, there were also rewards.

In conclusion, I've heard it said that, "Life is not about counting the years; rather, it is about making the years count." This, I believe, is true both at home and at work. I have also learned that life is not fair. There are forces beyond our control that impact our personal and work lives. Regardless, I believe there is much you can do to shape your future. How you react to the unforeseen and unexpected is important, and it, in large part, defines who you are. How you shape what you can control is just as important, if not more so.

I don't believe that our lives are preordained and strongly believe that we have great control over how we will be remembered and what our legacy will be. Do you want to count the years you spend at work or do you want the years to count? What do you want your legacy to be? Be a WARRIOR! TAKE THE HELM!

Acknowledgments

I first got the idea about this book about five years ago. At the time, my dear friend Dave McNally was still alive. When I started writing the book, I thought about Dave often. I thought about him because, beyond his friendship, he was someone who always inspired me to do better. Dave was a successful Chief Executive Officer at multiple companies, but, more important, he was a great husband, father and friend. He was also endowed with a heavy dose of irreverence about life and work that made him a lot of fun to be with. I miss him dearly and thank him for being an inspiration to me.

A special thanks to Mike Andres, an exemplary Warrior Leader, colleague and friend who twice saved me from making what could have been potentially disastrous career moves.

A special thanks also to four friends and colleagues who provided perspectives on the book and are Warriors in every sense of the word. Dave Thomas, Tom Kerestes, Chuck Zeisser and Brian Unger are all great Corporate Warrior Leaders and also served our country honorably as members of the military.

A heartfelt thanks to all my other friends, colleagues and Warriors who provided input and perspectives on the book, including Vicki Guster-Hines, Erica Navarro, John and Carmen Decarrier, Chris Delisa, Dave Daniels, Steve Russell, Jay Gillette, Rich Shields, Kim

Bayer, Gil Gomez, Tory Wozny, Marc Bigelow, Toni Poroda, Bill McKernan, Bud Lord, and Alma Anguiano.

I'm indebted to Cody Teets and Phyllis Hammond, who provided sound ideas about the book, and to Steve Plotkin for making my last five years before retirement a lot of fun.

To my dear friend Rebecca Young, whose recommendations and perspectives about the book were immeasurable. Thank you. I could not have done it without you!

I'm blessed that I crossed paths with Jon Tandler. His counsel, connections and insight were invaluable.

I am deeply grateful to my delightful and talented editor Susan Suffes for thoughtfully and thoroughly reviewing my work and making it better and to Michele, Ronda, Laura, Amy, Frank and the team at 1106 Design, who helped me through the last phase of publishing the book.

Much love to my wife and children, who endure a lot of dad's idiosyncrasies. Kyle, our son, and I have had many conversations about his experiences as a leader, and those conversations, in part, encouraged many of the ideas throughout the book. Our daughter, Michael, was the first to review the manuscript and to provide key suggestions. My lovely wife Randi has, from the day I met her, been an inspiration to me in many ways. As I tell her often, I love her so much it hurts, and I am forever indebted to her for her support.

Finally, there was one person in my life whose courage and determination gave our family the strength to persevere during our migration to the US. She did everything in her power to ensure my brother and I were set up for success; my mom Edelmira Marcos Rodriguez Pardo. She was also the kindest person I have ever known. *Gracias, viejita.*

Notes

Introduction

[1] Collins Jim, *Good to Great,* Harper Collins Publishers Inc, 2001, Chapter 2, "Level 5 Leadership"

[2] NBCNEWS.com, ENRON, *"Lay, Skilling Guilty on Nearly All Counts,"* Contributors Reuters and Associated press, Posted 25, May, 2006, Web, July 15, 2012

[3] USA TODAY, Money, *"Timeline of the Tyco International Scandal,"* Posted 5 June, 2005, USA TODAY research, Web, July 15, 2012

[4] The *New York Times* Archives, *"World-Com's Collapse: The overview; WorldCom Files for Bankruptcy; Largest US Case,"* By Simon Romero and Riva

Chapter One

[1] BIO. True Stories, *"Thomas Edison. Biography,"* Synopsis, Web, July 16, 2012

[2] BIO. True Stories, *"Abraham Lincoln.* Biography," Synopsis, Web, July 16, 2012

[3] BIO. True Stories, *"Clint Eastwood. Biography,"* Synopsis, Web, July 16, 2012

4 BIO. True Stories, *"Margaret Thatcher. Biography,"* Synopsis, Web, July 16, 2012

5 BIO. True Stories, *"George Washington Carver. Biography,"* Synopsis, Web, July 16, 2012

6 BIO. True Stories, *"Miguel De Cervantes. Biography,"* Synopsis, Web, July 16, 2012

7 BIO. True Stories, *"Amelia Earhart Biography,"* Synopsis, Web, July 16, 2012

8 Merriam-Webster.com, *"Occam's razor,"* Web, July 18, 2012

9 Vince Lombardi. *"Famous Quotes by Vince Lombardi,"* © 2010 Family of Vince Lombardi c/o Luminary Group LLC. Web July 28, 2012

Chapter Two

1 *The Economist,* "BP and Golden Parachutes; the wages of failure," 29, May, 2010 NEW YORK, from the print edition, Web, July 28, 2012

2 *The New York Daily News,* "BP's CEO Tony Hayward: The most hated — and most clueless — man in America," Helen Kennedy, *Daily News* Staff Writer, 2 June, 2010. Web, July 18, 2012

3 TIME, Lists *"25 People to Blame for the Financial Crisis: The Good Intentions, Bad Managers and Greed Behind the Meltdown,"* Web. July 18, 2012

4 NBCNEWS.com, *"The Enron Trail: Lay, Skilling Guilty on Nearly All Counts,"* Contributors Reuters and Associated press, Posted 25 May, 2006, Web, July 15, 2012

5 *TIME* Business and Money, *"How Fastow Helped Enron Fall,"* Reported by Cathy Booth Thomas/Dallas, Jyotti Thotton/Houston, Julie Rawe/New York and Michael Wesskopf/Washington, 10 May, 2002, Web July 18, 2012

[6] *Chicago Tribune, "Final Accounting: The Fall of Andersen,"* 1 September, 2002 Web July 18, 2012

[7] Churchill, Winston: selected by Churchill, Winston S. *"Never Give In! The Best of Winston Churchill's Speeches,"* New York: Hyperion 2003. p.218

[8] Churchill, Winston: selected by Churchill, Winston S. *"Never Give In! The Best of Winston Churchill's Speeches,"* New York: Hyperion 2003. p.221

[9] IlovetoKnow Business. *"Marketing Blunders,"* By Mary White. Web. August 5, 2012

[10] Marketing Translation Mistakes, *"Translations that (allegedly) embarrassed Their Marketing Departments,"* Acknowledgement: David A. Ricks' book *"Big Business Blunders—Mistakes in Multinational Marketing*[1], *(ISBN 0-256-02850-8, 1983 now out of print.) and Dave Taylor's Global Software,* Web, August 15

[11] Digital Dreams; A Member of Adventus. *"Famous Marketing Blunders,"* Copyright 2003. Web, August 5, 2012

[12] National Aeronautics and Space Administration: NASA History Office *"The Decision to Go to the Moon: President John F. Kennedy's May 25, 1961 Speech before a Joint Session of Congress"* Updated August 7, 2012 Steve Garber, NASA History Web Curator, Web, August 8, 2012

[13] Merriam-Webster.com, *"character,"* Web, August 8, 2012

Chapter Three

[1] US Department of Transportation National Highway Traffic, Safety and Transportation, DOT #S 811830, *"Distracted Driving and Driver Roadway and Environmental Factors,"* September 2010, Web, September 12, 2012

[2] History.com, "Challenger Disaster," Web, September 14, 2012

3 Aerospaceguide.net, "Space Shuttle Columbia Disaster," Web, September 14, 2012

4 Forbes.com, *"The Madoff Ponzi: Why the SEC Missed Madoff"* By Liz Moyer, 12.17.08, Web, September 14,2012

5 *The Washington Post* wit Bloomberg, "Madoff Sentenced to 150 Years", By Tomoeh Murakami Tse, June 30, 2009, Web, September 14, 2012

6 Washingtonpost.com, *"W. Va. coal mine to pay historic $209M settlement in blast that killed 29 miners,"* By Brad Plumer, December 06, 2011, Web, September 14,2012

7 AP/Huffington Post, "West Virginia Mine EXPLOSION: Massey Energy Mine Had Scores of Safety Citations," First Posted: 06/06/10, Updated: 05/25/11, Web, September 14, 2012

8 Tibbals, Geoff, *"Voices From The Titanic: The Epic Story of the Tragedy From the People Who Where There"* UK: Robinson, 2012 (paperback edition). P. X (Introduction)

9 Exxon Valdez Oil Spill Trustee Council, *"Oil Spill Facts: Questions and Answers,"* Web, September 12, 2012

10 The Telegraph.com.uk, *"Costa Concordia captain was in command of ship when it crashed,"* By Nick Squires, July 2012, Web, September 14 2012

11 BBC News Europe, *"Costa Concordia: Experts 'blame captain and firm,"* 13 September 2012, Web, September 14, 2012

12 ME: Maintenance and Asset Management, *"THE BHOPAL DISASTER: Learning from failures and evaluating risk,"* By Ashraf W. Labib and Ramesh Champaneri, May/June 2012, Web, September 14, 2012

13 The Franklin Institute: Resource for Science Learning, *"In Honor of Our Presidents,"* Web, October 1, 2012

[14] The Quotation Page, *"Quotations by Author Will Rogers (1879–1935), US humorist & showman,"* Web, October 2, 2012

Chapter Seven

[1] High Beam.com. *"Watergate Scandal"* By Joel Lee, Web, November 21, 2012

[2] YouTube.com, *"Clinton Denies the Lewinsky Affair,"* Uploaded August 30, 2006, Web, November 21, 2012

[3] YouTube.com, *"Bill Clinton admits to having inappropriate relationship with Monica Lewinsky,"* Uploaded on November 18, 2010, Web November 21,2012

Chapter Eight

[1] 1UP.com, *"What If Steve Jobs Had Never Returned to Apple?",* By Jeremy Parish, Week of May 21,2012, Web, November 22, 2012

Chapter Nine

[1] GoodReads.com, *"Voltaire Quotes,"* Web, November 23, 2012

[2] Investopedia.com, *"Definition of Dotcom Bubble,"* Web, November 23, 2012

[3] GoodReads.com, "Ben Franklin *Quotes,"* Web, November 30, 2012

[4] GoodReads.com, *"Thomas A. Edison Quotes,"* Web, November 23, 2012

[5] JustDisney.com, *"Walt Disney, Biography"* By Brad A., Web, November 30, 2012

[6] AgileWriter.com, *"Akio Morita, The founder of Sony,"* Biographies and History, By Ken Padgett, Web, November 30, 2012

[7] *Aol Jobs.com, "How Inner-City-Kid Farrah Gray Became A Millionaire By 14,"* By Dan Fastenberg, Posted Aug 24, 2011, Updated Aug 26, 2011, Web, November 30, 2012

8 GoodReads.com, *"Farrah Gray Quotes,"* Web, November 30, 2012

9 Tzu, Sun. Translated by Griffith, Samuel B. *"SUN TZU The Art of War."* London, Oxford and New York: Oxford University Press, 1963. Paperback edition p.84

31190844R00129

Made in the USA
Charleston, SC
09 July 2014